Interactive Computing Series

Microsoft® Word 2002 Brief Edition

Kenneth C. Laudon • Kenneth Rosenblatt

David Langley

Azimuth Interactive, Inc.

Interactive Computing Series

Microsoft® Word 2002 Brief Edition

Kenneth C. Laudon • Kenneth Rosenblatt
David Langley

Azimuth Interactive, Inc.

Boston   Burr Ridge, IL   Dubuque, IA   Madison, WI   New York   San Francisco   St. Louis
Bangkok   Bogotá   Caracas   Kuala Lumpur   Lisbon   London   Madrid   Mexico City
Milan   Montreal   New Delhi   Santiago   Seoul   Singapore   Sydney   Taipei   Toronto

McGraw-Hill Higher Education

A Division of The McGraw-Hill Companies

This book is printed on acid-free paper.

2 3 4 5 6 7 8 9 0 QPD/QPD 0 9 8 7 6 5 4 3 2

ISBN 0-07-247251-0

MICROSOFT WORD 2002 BRIEF EDITION
Published by McGraw-Hill/Irwin, an imprint of The McGraw-Hill Companies, Inc., 1221 Avenue of the Americas, New York, NY 10020. Copyright, 2002, by The McGraw-Hill Companies, Inc. All rights reserved. No part of this publication may be reproduced or distributed in any form or by any means, or stored in a database or retrieval system, without the prior written consent of The McGraw-Hill Companies, Inc., including, but not limited to, in any network or other electronic storage or transmission, or broadcast for distance learning.

Publisher: *George Werthman*
Developmental editor I: *Sarah Wood*
Senior marketing manager: *Jeff Parr*
Senior project manager: *Pat Frederickson*
Senior production supervisor: *Michael R. McCormick*
Coordinator freelance design: *Pam Verros*
Supplement producer: *Mark Mattson*
Cover illustration: *Kip Henrie*
Compositor: *Azimuth Interactive, Inc.*
Typeface: *10/12 Times*
Printer: *Quebecor Printing Book Group/Dubuque*

Library of Congress Control Number: 2001090813

www.mhhe.com

Information Technology at McGraw-Hill/Irwin

At McGraw-Hill Higher Education, we publish instructional materials targeted at the higher education market. In an effort to expand the tools of higher learning, we publish texts, lab manuals, study guides, testing materials, software, and multimedia products.

At McGraw-Hill/Irwin (a division of McGraw-Hill Higher Education), we realize that technology has created and will continue to create new mediums for professors and students to use in managing resources and communicating information with one another. We strive to provide the most flexible and complete teaching and learning tools available as well as offer solutions to the changing world of teaching and learning.

MCGRAW-HILL/IRWIN IS DEDICATED TO PROVIDING THE TOOLS FOR TODAY'S INSTRUCTORS AND STUDENTS TO SUCCESSFULLY NAVIGATE THE WORLD OF INFORMATION TECHNOLOGY.

- **Seminar series**—Technology Connection seminar series offered across the country every year demonstrates the latest technology products and encourages collaboration among teaching professionals.

- **Osborne/McGraw-Hill**—This division of The McGraw-Hill Companies is known for its best-selling Internet titles: Harley Hahn's Internet & Web Yellow Pages, and the Internet Complete Reference. Osborne offers an additional resource for certification and has strategic publishing relationships with corporations such as Corel Corporation and America Online. For more information visit Osborne at www.osborne.com.

- **Digital solutions**—McGraw-Hill/Irwin is committed to publishing digital solutions. Taking your course online does not have to be a solitary venture, nor does it have to be a difficult one. We offer several solutions that will allow you to enjoy all the benefits of having course material online. For more information visit www.mhhe.com/solutions/index.mhtml.

- **Packaging options**—For more about our discount options, contact your local McGraw-Hill/Irwin Sales representative at 1-800-338-3987 or visit our Web site at www.mhhe.com/it.

Interactive Computing Series

GOALS/PHILOSOPHY

The *Interactive Computing Series* provides you with an illustrated interactive environment for learning software skills using Microsoft Office. The text uses both "hands-on" instruction, supplementary text, and independent exercises to enrich the learning experience.

APPROACH

The *Interactive Computing Series* is the visual interactive way to develop and apply software skills. This skills-based approach coupled with its highly visual, two-page spread design allows the student to focus on a single skill without having to turn the page. A Lesson Goal at the beginning of each lesson prepares the student to apply the skills with a real-world focus. The Quiz and Interactivity sections at the end of each lesson measure the student's understanding of the concepts and skills learned in the two-page spreads and reinforce the skills with additional exercises.

ABOUT THE BOOK

The **Interactive Computing Series** offers *two levels* of instruction. Each level builds upon the previous level.

Brief lab manual—covers the basics of the application, contains two to four chapters.

Introductory lab manual—includes the material in the Brief textbook plus two to four additional chapters. The Introductory lab manuals prepare students for the *Microsoft Office User Specialist Proficiency Exam (MOUS Certification)*.

Each lesson is divided into a number of Skills. Each **Skill** is first explained at the top of the page in the Concept. Each **Concept** is a concise description of why the Skill is useful and where it is commonly used. Each **Step (Do It!)** contains the instructions on how to complete the Skill. The appearance of the **MOUS Skill** icon on a Skill page indicates that the Skill contains instruction in at least one of the required MOUS objectives for the relevant exam. Though the icons appear in the Brief manuals as well as the Introductory manuals, only the Introductory manuals may be used in preparation for MOUS Certification.

using the book

Figure 1

> WD 3.32 — LESSON THREE — Advanced Editing
>
> **skill** — **Finding and Replacing Text**
>
> **concept** — The Find command enables you to search a document for individual occurrences of any word, phrase, or other unit of text. The Replace command enables you to replace one or all occurrences of a word that you have found. Together, the Find and Replace commands form powerful editing tools for making many document-wide changes in just seconds.
>
> **do it!** — Use Find and Replace to spell a word consistently throughout a document.
>
> 1. Open student file, wddoit12.doc, and save it as Report12.doc.
> 2. If necessary, place the insertion point at the beginning of the document. Word will search the document from the insertion point forward.
> 3. Click Edit, and then click Replace. The Find and Replace dialog box appears with the Replace tab in front and the insertion point in the Find What text box.
> 4. In the Find What box, type the two words per cent. Click in the Replace With box, and type the one word percent (see Figure 3-37).
> 5. Click [Replace All] to search the document for all instances of per cent and to replace them with percent. A message box appears to display the results. In this case, one replacement was made (see Figure 3-38). In short documents the Find and Replace procedure takes so little time that you usually cannot cancel it before it ends. However, in longer documents you can cancel a search in progress by pressing [Esc].
> 6. Click [OK] to close the message box. Click [Close] to close the Find and Replace dialog box.
> 7. Save and close the document, Report12.doc, with your change.
>
> **more** — Clicking the Replace All button in the Find and Replace dialog box replaces every instance of the text you have placed in the Find What box. To examine and replace a word or phrase manually instead of automatically, start by clicking the Find Next button. If you desire to replace that instance, click the Replace button. Continue checking the document like this, clicking the Find Next button and then, if desired, the Replace button. Keep clicking the pairs of buttons until you have run through the entire document. Unless you absolutely must do otherwise, use the method for shorter documents only.
>
> The first button under the Replace With box usually displays the word More. Click this button when you want to display the Search Options area of the dialog box. With the area displayed, the More button converts to a Less button. Clicking on the Less button will hide the Search Options area. The Search drop-down list under Search Options determines the direction of the search relative to the insertion point. You can search upward or downward through the document or keep the Word default setting of All to check the whole document, including headers, footers, and footnotes. The Format drop-down list enables you to search criteria for fonts, paragraphs, tabs, and similar items. The Special drop-down list enables you to search for paragraph marks, tab characters, column breaks and related special characters. The No Formatting button removes all formatting criteria from searches. For information on the Search Option activated by the check boxes, consult Table 3-3.
>
> The Find tab of the Find and Replace dialog box matches the Replace tab except it lacks the replace function and only searches documents for items that you specify.

Skill: Each lesson is divided into a number of specific skills

Concept: A concise description of why the skill is useful and when it is commonly used

Do It!: Step-by-step directions show you how to use the skill in a real-world scenario

Hot Tips: Icons introduce helpful hints or troubleshooting tips

More: Provides in-depth information about the skill and related features

In the book, each skill is described in a two-page graphical spread (Figure 1). The left side of the two-page spread describes the skill, the concept, and the steps needed to perform the skill. The right side of the spread uses screen shots to show you how the screen should look at key stages.

Figure 1 (cont'd)

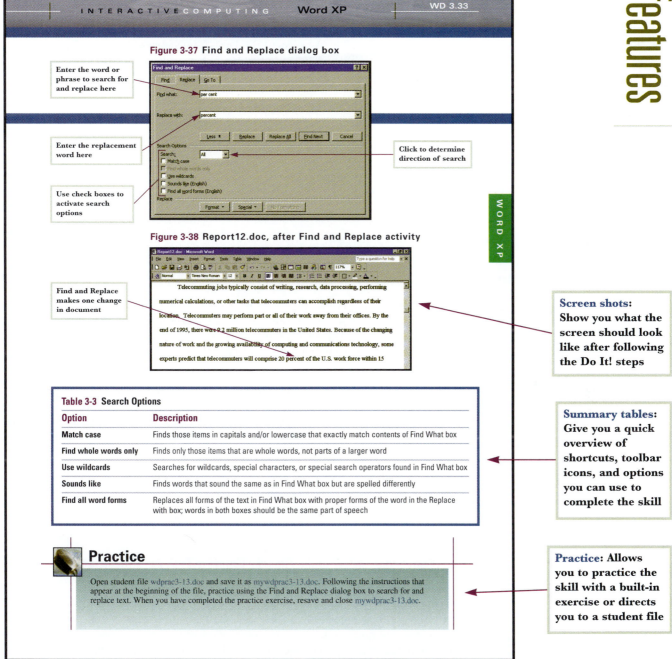

END-OF-LESSON FEATURES

In the book, the learning in each lesson is reinforced at the end by a Quiz and a skills review called Interactivity, which provides step-by-step exercises and real-world problems for the students to solve independently.

teaching resources

The following is a list of supplemental material available with the Interactive Computing Series:

Skills Assessment

SimNet eXPert (Simulated Network Assessment Product)—SimNet provides a way for you to test students' software skills in a simulated environment. SimNet is available for Microsoft Office 97, Microsoft Office 2000, and Microsoft Office XP. SimNet provides flexibility for you in your course by offering:

- Pre-testing options
- Post-testing options
- Course placement testing
- Diagnostic capabilities to reinforce skills
- Proficiency testing to measure skills
- Web or LAN delivery of tests
- Computer based training materials (New for Office XP)
- MOUS preparation exams
- Learning verification reports
- Spanish Version

Instructor's Resource Kits

The Instructor's Resource Kit provides professors with all of the ancillary material needed to teach a course. **McGraw-Hill/Irwin** is dedicated to providing instructors with the most effective instruction resources available. Many of these resources are available at our **Information Technology Supersite** www.mhhe.com/it. Our Instructor's Kits are available on CD-ROM and contain the following:

Diploma by Brownstone—is the most flexible, powerful, and easy-to-use computerized testing system available in higher education. The diploma system allows professors to create an Exam as a printed version, as a LAN-based Online version, and as an Internet version. Diploma includes grade book features, which automate the entire testing process.

Instructor's Manual—Includes:
–Solutions to all lessons and end-of-unit material
–Teaching Tips
–Teaching Strategies
–Additional exercises

PowerPoint Slides—NEW to the *Interactive Computing Series*, all of the figures from the application textbooks are available in PowerPoint slides for presentation purposes.

Student Data Files—To use the *Interactive Computing Series*, students must have Student Data Files to complete practice and test sessions. The instructor and students using this text in classes are granted the right to post the student files on any network or stand-alone computer, or to distribute the files on individual diskettes. The student files may be downloaded from our IT Supersite at www.mhhe.com/it.

Series Web Site—Available at www.mhhe.com/cit/apps/laudon.

Digital Solutions

Pageout—is our Course Web site Development Center. Pageout offers a Syllabus page, Web site address, Online Learning Center Content, online exercises and quizzes, gradebook, discussion board, an area for students to build their own Web pages, and all the features of Pageout Lite. For more information please visit the Pageout Web site at www.mhla.net/pageout.

Digital Solutions (continued)

OLC/Series Web Sites – Online Learning Centers (OLCs)/Series Sites are accessible through our Supersite at www.mhhe.com/it. Our Online Learning Centers/Series Sites provide pedagogical features and supplements for our titles online. Students can point and click their way to key terms, learning objectives, chapter overviews, PowerPoint slides, exercises, and Web links.

The McGraw-Hill Learning Architecture (MHLA) – is a complete course delivery system. MHLA gives professors ownership in the way digital content is presented to the class through online quizzing, student collaboration, course administration, and content management. For a walk-through of MHLA visit the MHLA Web site at www.mhla.net.

Packaging Options – For more about our discount options, contact your local McGraw-Hill/Irwin Sales representative at 1-800-338-3987 or visit our Web site at www.mhhe.com/it.

Visit www.mhhe.com/it
THE ONLY SITE WITH ALL YOUR CIT AND MIS NEEDS.

acknowledgments

The *Interactive Computing Series* is a cooperative effort of many individuals, each contributing to an overall team effort. The Interactive Computing team is composed of instructional designers, writers, multimedia designers, graphic artists, and programmers. Our goal is to provide you and your instructor with the most powerful and enjoyable learning environment using both traditional text and new interactive multimedia techniques. Interactive Computing is tested rigorously in both CD-ROM and text formats prior to publication.

Our special thanks to George Werthman, our Publisher; Sarah Wood, our Developmental Editor; and Jeffrey Parr, Marketing Director for Computer Information Systems. They have provided exceptional market awareness and understanding, along with enthusiasm and support for the project, and have inspired us all to work closely together. In addition, Steven Schuetz provided valuable technical review of our interactive versions, and Charles Pelto contributed superb quality assurance.

The Azimuth team members who contributed to the textbooks and CD-ROM multimedia program are:

Ken Rosenblatt (Editorial Director, Writer)
Russell Polo (Technical Director)
Steven D. Pileggi (Multimedia Project Director)
Robin Pickering (Developmental Editor, Writer)
Stefon Westry (Multimedia Designer)
Chris Hahnenberger (Multimedia Designer)
Joseph S. Gina (Multimedia Designer)
Irene Pileggi (Multimedia Designer)
Dan Langan (Multimedia Designer)
David Langley (Writer)

Interactive Computing Series

Microsoft® Word 2002 Brief Edition

contents

Word 2002 Brief Edition

Preface	**v**

LESSON ONE

Introduction to Word — WD 1.1

Starting Word	WD 1.2
Exploring the Word Screen	WD 1.4
Creating a Document and Entering Text ⓢ	WD 1.6
Saving and Closing a Document ⓢ	WD 1.8
Opening an Existing Document	WD 1.10
Deleting and Inserting Text ⓢ	WD 1.12
Formatting Text ⓢ	WD 1.14
Previewing and Printing a Document ⓢ	WD 1.16
Shortcuts	WD 1.18
Quiz	WD 1.19
Interactivity	WD 1.21

LESSON TWO

Editing Documents — WD 2.1

Searching for Files	WD 2.2
Selecting Text and Undoing Actions	WD 2.4
Cutting, Copying, and Moving Text ⓢ	WD 2.6
Copying and Moving Text with the Mouse ⓢ	WD 2.8
Creating a Document with a Wizard ⓢ	WD 2.10
Creating a Document with a Template ⓢ	WD 2.14
Using the Office Assistant	WD 2.18
Other Word Help Features	WD 2.20
Shortcuts	WD 2.22
Quiz	WD 2.23
Interactivity	WD 2.25

ⓢ Skill covers at least one MOUS Certification objective.

Word 2002 continued

LESSON THREE

Advanced Editing — WD 3.1

Setting Up a Page ⓢ	WD 3.2
Inserting Page Numbers ⓢ	WD 3.4
Inserting Footnotes and Endnotes ⓢ	WD 3.6
Applying Paragraph Indents ⓢ	WD 3.8
Changing Line Spacing ⓢ	WD 3.10
Inserting Page Breaks ⓢ	WD 3.12
Working with Multiple Documents ⓢ	WD 3.14
Using the Format Painter	WD 3.16
Checking Spelling and Grammar ⓢ	WD 3.18
Using AutoCorrect	WD 3.22
Inserting Frequently Used Text ⓢ	WD 3.26
Using the Word Thesaurus ⓢ	WD 3.30
Finding and Replacing Text ⓢ	WD 3.32
Shortcuts	WD 3.34
Quiz	WD 3.35
Interactivity	WD 3.37

LESSON FOUR

Tables and Charts — WD 4.1

Creating and Modifying Tables ⓢ	WD 4.2
Editing Tables ⓢ	WD 4.6
Inserting and Deleting Rows, Columns, and Cells ⓢ	WD 4.8
Sorting Data in a Table	WD 4.10
Calculating Data in a Table ⓢ	WD 4.12
Formatting a Table ⓢ	WD 4.16
Creating a Chart ⓢ	WD 4.18
Editing a Chart ⓢ	WD 4.20
Drawing a Table ⓢ	WD 4.22
Adding Borders and Shading ⓢ	WD 4.26
Shortcuts	WD 4.30
Quiz	WD 4.31
Interactivity	WD 4.33

Glossary — WD 1

Index — WD 9

File Directory — WD 12

ⓢ Skill covers at least one MOUS Certification objective.

Introduction to Word

Microsoft Word 2002 is the latest edition of Microsoft's powerful word processing software application. It is designed to make the creation of professional-quality documents fast and easy. Word processing software allows you to type the text of a document electronically and edit, move, and stylize that text, even after it has been written. Word processors provide enormous flexibility in how the finished product will appear.

Word's capabilities are not limited to text. As features have been added through the various generations of the program, it has gained the capacity to serve as a desktop publishing tool. Among many other features, Word will let you:

- Copy, move, and change the appearance of text within a document
- Share text and other page elements among documents
- Create documents using ready-made templates
- Add page numbers and footnotes to documents automatically
- Find and correct spelling and grammar errors automatically
- Insert tables, charts, and pictures in your documents
- Request help while you are using the program
- Search for specific instances of text and formatting within a document
- See how your document will appear on paper before printing it

Starting Word
Exploring the Word Screen
Creating a Document and Entering Text
Saving and Closing a Document
Opening an Existing Document
Deleting and Inserting Text
Formatting Text
Previewing and Printing a Document

While you work on a document, it is stored in your computer's temporary memory. In order to keep a document permanently so you can work with it again, Word enables you to save it as a file on a storage device such as a floppy disk or hard disk drive. You can use Word to create everything from a one-page business letter to a book containing thousands of pages.

Lesson Goal:

Create a cover letter that will accompany a résumé a student is sending in order to apply for a job.

skill: Starting Word

concept

The first step in using the Microsoft Word program, or application, is launching it. The Windows operating system provides a number of ways to launch programs. When you install Word (or Microsoft Office, the suite of programs of which Word is a part), a shortcut to the program is placed on the Windows Start menu automatically. You can also open Word by locating and running its executable file, named Winword.exe, through My Computer or Windows Explorer.

do it!

Use the Start menu to launch the Microsoft Word application.

1. Turn on your computer and monitor and make sure that any peripheral devices such as your mouse are connected properly. When your edition of the Windows operating system finishes loading, the Windows desktop should appear on your screen (you may be asked to provide a user name and password before Windows finishes loading).

2. Click the Start button  on the Windows taskbar at the bottom of your screen. The Windows Start menu will appear.

3. Move the mouse pointer up the Start menu to the Programs folder. The Programs submenu will open beside the Start menu.

4. Move the mouse pointer over to the Programs submenu from the Start menu, and point to Microsoft Word. The program name will be highlighted, as shown in Figure 1-1. Newer editions of the Windows operating system such as Windows Me use personalized menus, which means that only the items you use most frequently are displayed on a menu when it first opens. If Personalized menus are active on your computer and you do not see Microsoft Word listed on the Programs menu, click the double arrow at the bottom of the menu to display the rest of the program listings.

5. Click the left mouse button once. Word will open with a blank document in the window (see Figure 1-2). If your copy of Word has been used previously, the appearance of the application window may differ from the one shown in the figure.

more

Do not be alarmed if your desktop or Start menu do not match the descriptions above or the figures on the next page exactly. With several different versions of Windows and countless software applications available, variances in system configuration are more than likely. Windows itself is highly customizable, so the location or appearance of items such as the taskbar and the desktop are also subject to change. Furthermore, you can customize the way in which you interact with the operating system. For example, you can alter the functionality of the mouse so that tasks that normally require a double-click only require a single click. For the purposes of this book, the term click means to press and release the left mouse button quickly. When instructed to double-click, you should press and release the left mouse button twice in rapid succession. A right-click instruction requires you to press and release the right mouse button once. Finally, click and drag means to press and hold the left mouse button down, move the mouse as instructed, and then release the mouse button to complete the action.

Figure 1-1 Opening Word from the Start menu

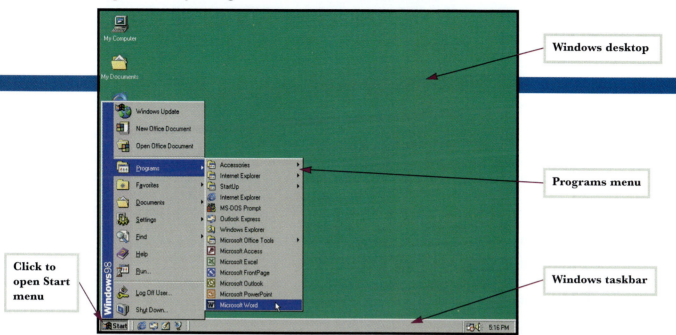

Figure 1-2 Word application window

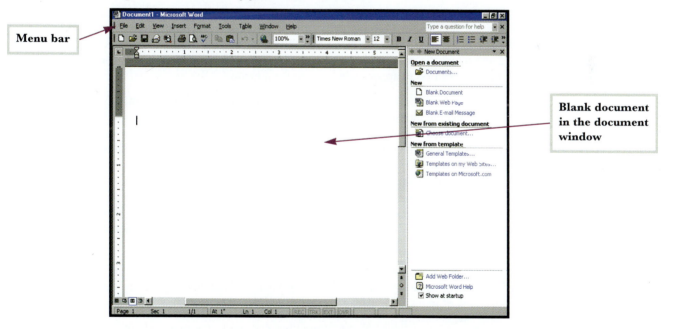

Practice

Click the File menu title on the Menu bar. The File menu will drop down below its menu title. Move the mouse pointer down the File menu and click the Exit command to close the Word application. If you do not see the Exit command, click the double arrow at the bottom of the menu to expand the menu. When you have successfully exited Word, use the Start menu to open the application again.

skill: Exploring the Word Screen

concept

The Word application window consists of many features that are common to all applications running under the Windows operating system. These include a Title bar, a Menu bar, document and window control buttons, and toolbars. In addition to these items, Word has many unique features that are designed to make document production fast, flexible, and convenient. The main components of the Word window are shown in Figure 1-3 and are described below.

 Figure 1-3 displays Word in a maximized window set to Print Layout View with the Task Pane open. If your screen does not look like the figure, you can click View on the Menu bar to access commands that will allow you to switch to Print Layout View, activate the Task Pane, and set the Zoom level to 100%.

The Title bar shows the name of the active document and the name of the application. New documents are named Document1, Document2, etc., until they are saved with a new name.

The Menu bar displays the titles of the menus containing Word commands. Clicking one of these titles will make its menu appear, listing the commands from which you can choose. Word 2002 uses personalized menus by default, so only a few commands may appear when you first open a menu. These are the commands that have been deemed most popular by the designers of the software. If you do not click one of the available commands, the menu will expand after a few seconds to reveal more commands. You can expedite this expansion by clicking the double arrow at the bottom of the menu or by clicking the menu title again. Alternatively, double-click the menu title to open the full menu right away. As you use Word more and more, the program learns which commands you use most often. These commands will then be the first to appear when you open a menu.

The Standard toolbar contains buttons that serve as shortcuts to commonly used commands. When you rest the mouse pointer over a button, a ScreenTip that describes the button's function appears. The Formatting toolbar contains the Font and Font Size boxes along with many other options for formatting text and inserted objects. Overall, Word provides numerous other toolbars to help you complete your tasks. Some of these toolbars will appear automatically when you execute certain commands. You can activate any toolbar manually by opening the View menu, highlighting the Toolbars command, and then clicking the name of the toolbar you want to display on the Toolbars submenu. You hide an active toolbar by clicking its name again on the submenu. You may also click and drag toolbars to change their order, or click and drag them to other locations in the window.

In Print Layout View, the document window includes both a horizontal ruler and a vertical ruler. The rulers enable you to keep track of your position on the page and view and change the locations of items such as page margins, indents, tabs, columns, and table gridlines.

The insertion point is the blinking vertical bar that marks the place where text will appear when it is entered, or where an object will be placed when it is inserted.

The document window is the open space in which your document appears. When the mouse pointer is within the borders of the document it changes from the standard pointing arrow to an I-beam I so you can position it in text more accurately.

The Task Pane, which occupies the right side of the application window in the default setup, is a new feature. It helps you organize your most important Word tasks in a single location. The content of the Task Pane changes depending on the actions you are performing. For example, there are different Task Panes for searching, formatting, and opening documents.

In the current view, a vertical scroll bar appears on the right side of the document window, and a horizontal scroll bar is found at the bottom of the window. The position of the scroll bar boxes within the scroll bars indicates where the visible text is located in relation to the portions of the document that are not currently visible on the screen. Clicking the scroll arrows at the ends of the scroll bars advances the document in small increments. Clicking in the scroll bar itself, above or below the scroll bar box, advances the document in larger increments. You can also click and drag the scroll box within the scroll bar to move substantial distances in a document (such as several pages at once).

The Status bar at the bottom of the application window provides feedback about your current activity in Word. The left most section tells you what page and section of your document is currently displayed in the document window. It also indicates the total number of pages in the document. The next section shows the distance the insertion point is from the top of the page and its position on the page in terms of Line and Column number. The third portion of the Status bar is reserved for showing whether certain Word modes such as Overtype and Track Changes are active.

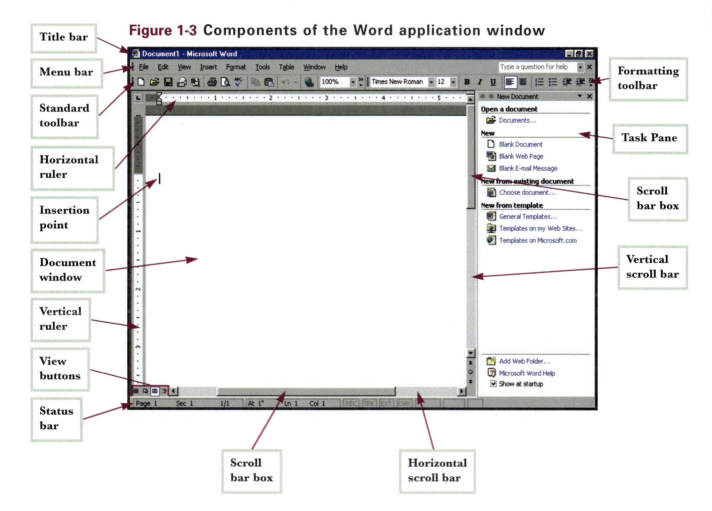

Figure 1-3 Components of the Word application window

Practice

As shown in the figure above, the Standard and Formatting toolbars are arranged in a single row by default. This setting gives you more screen space for your document, but limits the number of buttons you can see on each of the toolbars. The double arrow pointing to the right at the end of the toolbar indicates that more buttons are available. The downward-pointing arrow indicates that a menu will appear if you click the arrows. Click a set of arrows and then click Show Buttons on Two Rows. The Formatting toolbar will move below the Standard toolbar so you have a better view of both toolbars.

Creating a Document and Entering Text

concept

Data that you enter in Word becomes part of an electronic file also known as a document. You must have a document open in order to begin word processing. When you open the Word application, a new blank document appears in the document window automatically. In Print Layout View, the document is designed to look like an actual piece of paper.

do it!

Type a name and address in a new Word document to begin a letter.

1. Assuming you have already opened Word, a new document should be in the document window with Document1 in the Title bar. You can also create a new document when Word is running by clicking the New Blank Document button on the Standard toolbar.

2. Use the keyboard to type the following text, pressing [Enter] after each line as indicated:

    Sabrina Lee [Enter]
    12 Oakleigh Ave. [Enter]
    Indianapolis, IN 46202 [Enter]

3. The text will appear at the insertion point as you are typing it. When you are finished, your document should look like Figure 1-4.

4. Leave the document open for use in the next Skill.

more

In this exercise, you pressed [Enter] after each line of text to begin a new one because an address consists of short, distinct lines. When typing a document that does not require abbreviated lines, you do not have to press [Enter] to begin a new line. Word uses a feature known as Word Wrap to continue the text on the next line when you run out of space on the current line. When a word is too long to fit on the current line, it is placed at the beginning of the line below, allowing you to type without interruptions or guesswork.

You may have noticed that some words have wavy red lines or purple dots beneath them. The wavy red lines indicate that Word's Automatic Spell Checking feature is active, and the underlined words are not recognized by Word's dictionary. You will learn how to spell check later in this book. Purple dots below a word or phrase indicate a Smart Tag. In this example, Word has recognized "12 Oakleigh Ave." as an address. If you place the I-beam mouse pointer over the purple underline, a Smart Tag button will appear. When you click the Smart Tag button, a menu containing commands related specifically to working with addresses will appear. Smart Tags will appear in a variety of circumstances, including when you type names, dates, Web addresses, and e-mail addresses. In each case, you can access a context-sensitive menu by clicking the smart tag button, giving you control over operations in Word that usually involve using another program such as an address book or e-mail client.

In addition to launching Word or clicking a toolbar button, you can create a new document by clicking Blank Document in the New section of the New Document Task Pane (see Figure 1-5). From the Task Pane, you can also create new documents from existing ones and new documents from templates. For now, you will learn to use general blank documents. Other types of documents and methods of document creation will be covered in later lessons. Some commands have shortcut key combinations associated with them. Pressing these key combinations on the keyboard is the same as executing the command from a toolbar or from the Task Pane. For example, the keyboard shortcut [Ctrl]+[N] creates a new document (the Ctrl key must remain pressed while you press N). If your Task Pane is hidden, clicking the New command on the File menu will open the New Document Task Pane.

Figure 1-4 Entering Text in Word

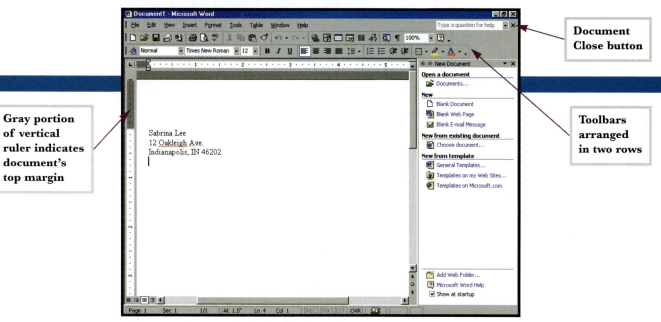

Figure 1-5 New Document Task Pane

Practice

Click the New Blank Document button 🗋 on the Standard toolbar. A new document will open in its own Word window. Type your name and address in the new document as if you were writing a letter. When you are done, click the Document Close button ✖ (the lower of the two buttons marked with an X) on the right end of the Menu bar to remove this practice document from the screen. When Word asks if you would like to save the document, click the button labeled No.

LESSON ONE — Introduction to Word

 ## Saving and Closing a Document

concept

It is essential to save documents by giving them unique names and locations on a storage device such as a floppy disk or hard disk. Otherwise, your work will be lost when you exit Word. It is also a good idea to save documents periodically as you work on them to minimize the amount of data lost due to power or computer failures. Closing a document removes it from the screen and "files it away," if you choose to save it, so you can retrieve it and continue working with it later. You can close individual documents and still leave Word running so you can work on other documents.

do it!

Save the name and address you typed in the previous Skill as a file and then close the file.

1. You should still have the name and address you typed in the previous Skill on your screen. Click File, then click Save As to open the Save As dialog box. When you are saving a document for the first time, the Save As dialog box will appear regardless of whether you have chosen the Save command or the Save As command. The Save As dialog box allows you to provide a file with a particular file name and select the location where the file will be saved. Once a file has been saved, the Save and Save As commands have different functions. Using the Save command or the Save button on the Standard toolbar will overwrite the old version of the file with the current version, without opening a dialog box. Using the Save As command will open the Save As dialog box, allowing you to save another version of the file with either a new file name, a new storage location, or both.

2. When the Save As dialog box opens, Word provides a suggested file name based on the initial text you have typed in the document. This default name is highlighted in the File name box, so you can replace it simply by typing a new name. Type Address.doc to replace the default file name. .doc is the file extension for Word documents. A file extension identifies a file as a certain type and associates the file with a specific program.

3. Word's default storage location is your computer's My Documents folder, which you can see selected near the top of the dialog box in the Save in drop-down list box. You can select a different location by clicking the Save in box to open its drop-down list, or by clicking one of the buttons on the Places bar on the left side of the dialog box. (For example, if you are to save your files on a floppy disk instead of the hard drive, insert the disk, open the Save in drop-down list, and click 3½ Floppy (A:) before continuing.) You also can create new folders for your documents. Click the Create New Folder button to the right of the Save in box. The New Folder dialog box appears, as shown in Figure 1-6.

4. Type Word Files in the Name text box as the name of the new folder, and then click the OK button. The folder is created and selected immediately in the Save in box. The dialog box should now look like Figure 1-7. The folder you just created is a subfolder of the My Documents folder, since that folder was selected in the Save in box when you clicked the Create New Folder button.

5. Click the Save button in the bottom-right corner of the dialog box to save the Address.doc file in the Word Files folder. The dialog box will close and the document remains on the screen. Notice that the file name you provided in the Save As dialog box now appears in the Title bar.

6. Click the Close button on the right end of the Menu bar to close the active document, Address.doc, but leave the Word application running.

more

If you modify a document and do not save the changes before you close it, Word will open a dialog box that asks you if you want to save the changes. If you do not save, any changes you have made since the last time you saved the document will be lost when the document closes.

You have probably noticed that there are two similar-looking Close buttons in the upper-right corner of the Word window. The lower Close button ⊠ (as it appears with the mouse pointer resting over it), which sits by itself on the right end of the Menu bar, is used for closing the active document. The upper Close button ⊠, located on the Title bar, closes the application itself. If you have documents with unsaved changes open when you click the application Close button, you will be prompted to save the changes. Next to the application Close button are two buttons that help you control the size of the application window. Clicking the Minimize button ▭ hides the window from view, leaving only its program button on the taskbar. The middle button changes depending on the current size of the window. When the window is maximized, you will see the Restore button ▭ which reduces the window to its last smaller size. When the window is reduced, you will see the Maximize button ▭, which increases the size of the window so that it fills the screen. You can also access window control commands by clicking the Word Control menu icon 🅦 on the left end of the Title bar.

Figure 1-6 New Folder dialog box

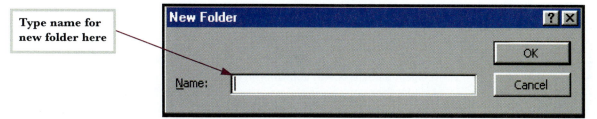

Type name for new folder here

Figure 1-7 Save As dialog box

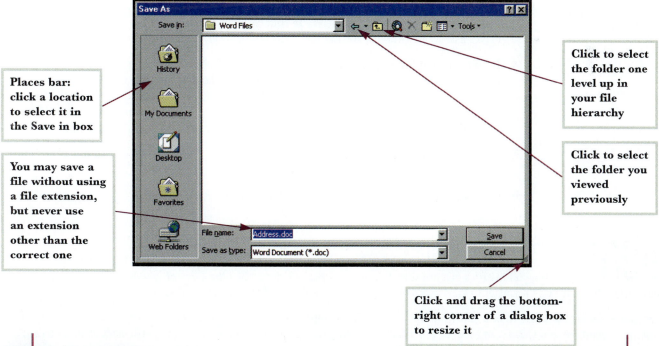

Places bar: click a location to select it in the Save in box

You may save a file without using a file extension, but never use an extension other than the correct one

Click to select the folder one level up in your file hierarchy

Click to select the folder you viewed previously

Click and drag the bottom-right corner of a dialog box to resize it

Practice

Open a new document and type a short paragraph about how learning Word will be helpful to you. When you are finished writing, save the document in your Word Files folder using the file name Saving and Closing.doc. Then close the document but leave Word open.

skill — Opening an Existing Document

concept

To view or edit a document that has been saved and closed previously, you must open the document from the location in which it was stored. Since Word documents are associated with the Word application by the .doc file extension in their file names, you can double-click a Word document in My Computer or Windows Explorer and Word will launch automatically. However, if you are already working in Word, you can open Word files from directly within the application. If the Student Files that accompany this book have been distributed to you on a floppy disk, make sure you have inserted the disk in your floppy drive for this Skill.

do it !

Open an existing Word document that was previously saved on a floppy disk or hard disk.

1. With the Word application running, click the Open button on the Standard toolbar. The Open dialog box will appear. The Open dialog is constructed very similarly to the Save As dialog box you saw in the previous Skill. You also can access the Open dialog box by clicking File on the Menu bar and then clicking the Open command on the File menu.

2. Click the Look in drop-down list box. A list of locations available on your computer will appear, as shown in Figure 1-8.

3. If your Student Files are stored on a floppy disk, click 3½ Floppy (A:) on the drop-down list to select your floppy disk drive. If your Student Files are stored on a local or network drive, ask your instructor for the name of the location you should select.

4. If your Student Files are stored in a folder on your floppy disk or hard disk, you will need to double-click that folder to display its contents in the dialog box's Contents window. Otherwise, you should already see a list of files in the Contents window. Click the file named wddoit1-5.doc to select it. It is possible that your computer is set to hide file extensions of known file types, in which case you will see a file named wddoit1-5.

5. Click the Open button in the bottom-right corner of the dialog box. The Word file wddoit1-5 will appear in the document window.

6. Click ✗ on the right end of the Menu bar to close the document.

more

Word can open a variety of file types in addition to the standard Word document (.doc). Which files appear in the Open dialog box depends on the setting in the Files of type box. To ensure that you are seeing all the files that are stored in the selected directory, click the Files of type box and select the All Files (*.*) setting. If you only want to view Word documents, select the Word Documents (*.doc) setting.

If you click the arrow on the right edge of the Open button in the Open dialog box, a menu appears that offers commands for opening a document in a specific manner. If you select Open Read-Only, Word will not allow any permanent changes to be made to the document during that particular work session unless you use Save As to save the document as a new file. Otherwise, you can edit the text on your screen and print, but you will not be able to save the changes. The Open as Copy command creates a new copy of your document, allowing you to keep the old version and edit the new one. The Open in Browser command becomes active when you have selected an HTML document in the Contents window. Executing this command enables you to view the document with your default Web browser instead of Word. Finally, use the Open and Repair command to open and recover a document that has been damaged by a program, system, or power failure.

Files that you have worked with recently appear at the bottom of the File menu and on the Task Pane so you can open them without having to go through the Open dialog box (see Figure 1-9).

Figure 1-8 Open dialog box

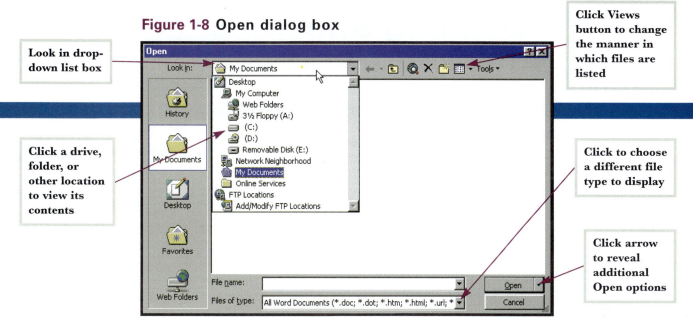

Figure 1-9 Opening recent documents

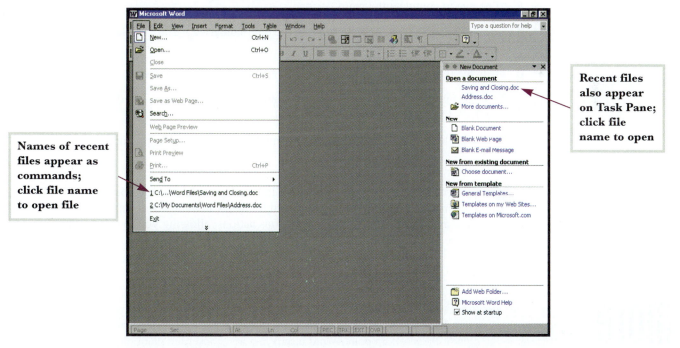

Practice

To practice opening a document, open the Student File named wdprac1-5.doc. Type a few sentences explaining the steps you used to open the file. Then use the Save As command to save the file in your Word Files folder using the name mywdprac1-5.doc (to change the file name in the Save As dialog box, you do not need to delete the entire name and then type the new one; simply click in front of the original name and type my). Close the file and leave Word running when you are done.

skill Deleting and Inserting Text

concept

One of the fundamental advantages of word processing is the ease with which it enables you to change content that has been entered previously. Word makes it easy to edit, replace, or delete unwanted or inaccurate text. Editing skills are crucial for updating older documents and making revisions that will turn your rough drafts into final drafts.

do it!

Modify text in an existing document.

1. Open the Student File wddoit1-6.doc. In the Open dialog box, you can open a file by double-clicking it instead of clicking it once and then clicking the Open button.

2. Move the I-beam mouse pointer to the immediate right of the abbreviation Ave. in the second line of the address at the top of the document. Click to place the insertion point at the end of the line.

3. Press [Backspace] on the keyboard once to erase the period.

4. Type nue to complete the word Avenue.

5. Click between the two and the three in the date January 23, 2002 to place the insertion point between the two numbers.

6. Press the [Delete] key on the keyboard to erase the number three.

7. Type the number 4 on the keyboard to complete the date change. The document should now look like the one shown in Figure 1-10.

8. Save the file in your Word Files folder using the file name Deleting and Inserting.doc.

9. Close the file.

If you make a mistake while working in Word, you can reverse your last action by clicking the Undo button on the Standard toolbar. Click the arrow next to the Undo button to open a menu that lists all of your previous actions, allowing you to undo multiple actions at once (see Figure 1-11).

more

As you just saw, the [Backspace] key (some keyboards spell it Back Space and some only use a left-pointing arrow) erases the character immediately to the left of the insertion point. The [Delete] key erases the character to the right of the insertion point. Word inserts text at the insertion point; that is, it moves nearby text to the right instead of typing over it. To type over existing text so that it disappears instead of moving, double-click the Overtype button OVR on the Status bar to enter Overtype mode. Just remember that any text to the right of the insertion point will be deleted as you type. Double-click the Overtype button again to deactivate Overtype mode.

You can move the insertion point one character at a time to the left or right and one line at a time up or down with the arrow keys on the keyboard. This is especially helpful when you are moving the insertion point only a short distance. Additional ways to move the insertion point using the keyboard are shown in Table 1-1. If you will be using the [Home], [End], [Pg Up], and [Pg Dn] keys on the numeric keypad, as required for some of the movement techniques described in the table, make sure that Num Lock is disabled. Many keyboards now include separate keys for these functions.

Figure 1-10 Document after editing

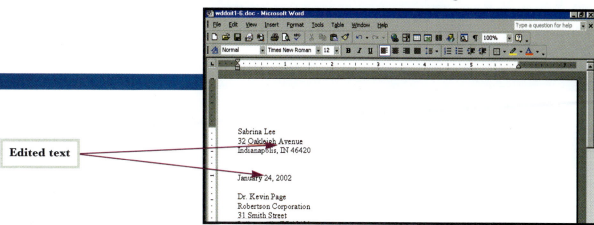

Figure 1-11 Undoing multiple actions

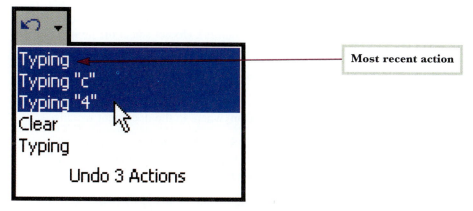

Table 1-1 Moving the insertion point with the keyboard

To Move the Insertion Point	Press
Left or right one word	[Ctrl]+[←] or [Ctrl]+[→]
Up or down one paragraph	[Ctrl]+[↑] or [Ctrl]+[↓]
Up or down one screen	[Pg Up] or [Pg Dn]
To the beginning or end of a line	[Home] or [End]
To the beginning or end of a document	[Ctrl]+[Home] or [Ctrl]+[End]

Practice

To practice inserting and deleting text, open the Student File **wdprac1-6.doc** and follow the instructions given in the file. When you are finished, save the file in your Word Files folder as **mywdprac1-6.doc** and close the file.

skill Formatting Text

concept

Word enables you to easily change the font (typeface), font size, text style, and text alignment in a document, as well as many other text and document characteristics. Formatting text serves to improve the presentation of your document. You can format text for both stylistic and organizational purposes.

do it!

Apply bold formatting to text in a letter and change the font size of the document.

1. Open the Student File wddoit1-7.doc.
2. Select Assistant to the Director of Public Relations in the first paragraph of the letter by clicking before the A and dragging (moving the mouse with the left mouse button held down) to the end of Relations (release the mouse button). Do not select the period. The selected text will be white on a black background.
3. Click the Bold button **B** on the Formatting toolbar. The letters in the job title will be set in a heavier text style.
4. Cancel the selection of the text by clicking once anywhere in the document window.
5. Select the entire document by clicking before the S in Sabrina at the top of the letter and dragging down to the last line (release the mouse button after the period in enc.). You also can select an entire document by pressing the keyboard shortcut [Ctrl]+[A].
6. Click the Font Size arrow [12 ▼] on the Formatting toolbar. A list of font sizes will appear. Click 10, as shown in Figure 1-12. The document text decreases in size.
7. Click the Font arrow [Times New Roman ▼], and then click the font named Arial on the drop-down list (you may have to scroll up the list of fonts). The typeface of the document changes to the Arial font.
8. Deselect the text as you did above and scroll to the top of the document.
9. Save the document in your Word Files folder as Formatting Text.doc and close it.

more

The Formatting toolbar allows you to change numerous text attributes. Font, or typeface, refers to the actual shape of each individual character as it appears on the screen or in a printed document. Font size is usually measured in points, with 72 points being equivalent to one inch. As an example, the text in a newspaper is generally 10-point type. Other Formatting toolbar options include Italic [*I*], Underline [U], Font Color [A▼], and Highlight [✎▼]. The Font Color and Highlight buttons are always loaded with a color, which is indicated as part of the button icon. Clicking the buttons applies the formatting with the loaded color. Clicking the arrow next to the buttons opens a color palette, enabling you to select a different color. Another formatting option, Alignment, refers to the manner in which text follows the margins of your document (see Figure 1-13). Like the Italic, Underline, and Bold buttons, the Alignment buttons are toggle buttons, meaning that you can apply and remove their formatting by clicking the same button.

Knowing how to format text for maximum effect is an essential skill that will make your documents appear crisp and professional. Notice how formatting is used on this page: different fonts and font sizes are used for headings and subject matter and important terms are colored for added emphasis. As you saw above, you must select items before you can format them. Note that you also can select an entire document by opening the Edit menu and clicking the Select All command. You can align an entire paragraph simply by placing the insertion point inside the paragraph before clicking the desired alignment button.

Figure 1-12 Changing font size

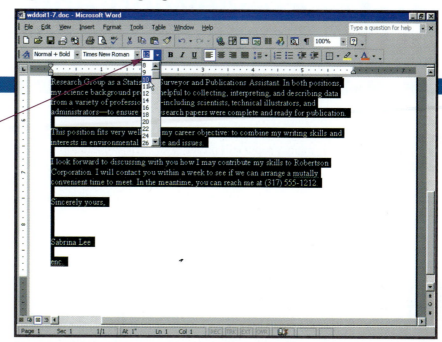

You also may click in the Font Size box, type a font size, and press [Enter] to apply it

Figure 1-13 Text alignment

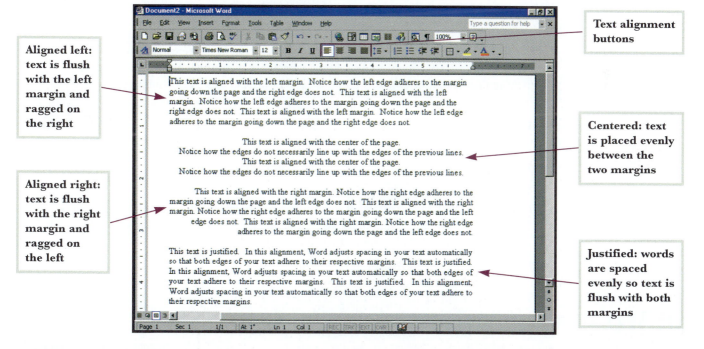

Aligned left: text is flush with the left margin and ragged on the right

Aligned right: text is flush with the right margin and ragged on the left

Text alignment buttons

Centered: text is placed evenly between the two margins

Justified: words are spaced evenly so text is flush with both margins

Practice

To practice formatting text, open the Student File **wdprac1-7.doc** and follow the instructions given in the file. When you have completed the exercise, save the file in your Word Files folder as **mywdprac1-7.doc**. Then close the file.

skill Previewing and Printing a Document

concept

While today's classrooms and offices are relying more and more on electronic documents, many people still prefer to work with hard copies (paper printouts) out of their documents. If your computer is properly connected to a printer, you can print a paper copy of a document with a click of a button. Or, if you desire more flexibility in printing, Word provides comprehensive printing options, including a Print Preview that allows you to see the document as it will appear when printed.

do it!

Preview and print a document.

1. Open the Student File wddoit1-8.doc and type your name at the top of the document.

2. Click the Print Preview button on the Standard toolbar. The open document will appear in Preview mode. The reduced size of the document allows you to view how your text is arranged on the page.

3. Move the mouse pointer over the upper-left corner of the document. The pointer should appear as the Magnifier tool, as shown in Figure 1-14. If the Magnifier tool is not present, click the Magnifier button on the Print Preview toolbar.

4. Click the upper-left corner of the document with the Magnifier tool. The preview will zoom in to 100% so you can see the document at its normal size. Notice that the Magnifier tool now contains a minus symbol instead of a plus symbol. Click again to zoom back out.

5. Click the Close button on the Print Preview toolbar to return to the regular document window.

6. Click File on the Menu bar, then click the Print command. The Print dialog box appears, as shown in Figure 1-15.

7. Click the OK button to print the document with the default print settings. Clicking the Print button on the Standard toolbar skips the dialog box and prints using the default print settings automatically.

8. Close the document. You do not need to save it.

more

For more precise control over your view in Print Preview mode, click the Zoom box arrow 42% to open a list of magnification percentages. Then click a percentage on the drop-down list. The percentages are based on 100% being the actual size of the document. To select a Zoom percentage that is not on the list, click the current value in the Zoom box, type a new percentage, and press [Enter] on the keyboard.

To edit a document while in Print Preview mode, click the Magnifier button to toggle it off. The mouse pointer will change to an I-beam. You then can enter and edit text as you normally would.

While Print Layout View affords you many of the same advantages as Print Preview mode, Print Preview includes some very useful and unique features. For example, you can choose to view multiple pages of a document on the same screen by clicking the Multiple Pages button on the Print Preview toolbar. You also can reduce by one the number of pages in a document by clicking the Shrink to Fit button so that a small portion of text is not left alone on one page. Word accomplishes this reduction by decreasing the font sizes used in the document.

Figure 1-14 Print Preview mode

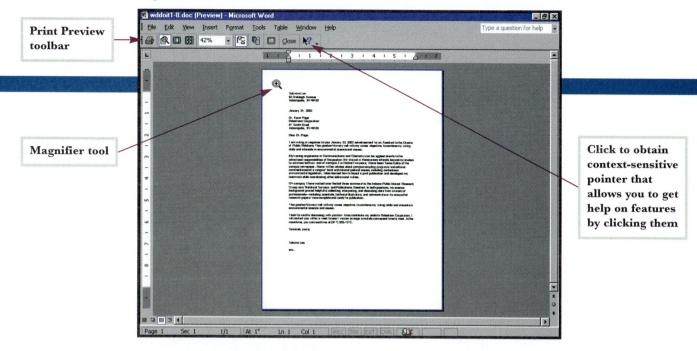

Figure 1-15 Print dialog box

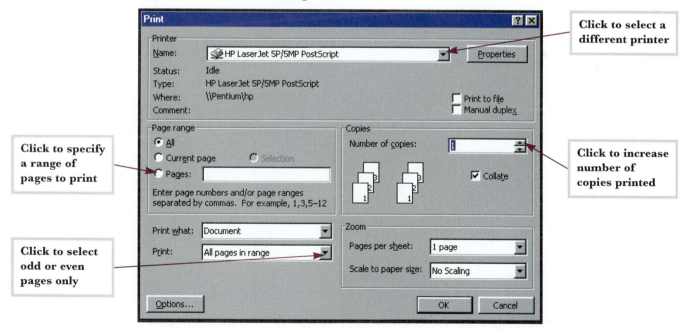

Practice

To practice previewing and printing a document, open the Student File wdprac1-8.doc. Type your name below the title of the document, and then preview and print the file as instructed. When you have completed the exercise, close the file. You do not have to save the file.

shortcuts

Function	Button/Mouse	Menu	Keyboard
Create new document		Click File, then click New	[Ctrl]+[N]
Close active document		Click File, then click Close	[Ctrl]+[W]
Save document for the first time		Click File, then click Save or Save As	[Ctrl]+[S]
Save changes to existing document		Click File, then click Save	[Ctrl]+[S]
Save document with new name and/or location		Click File, then click Save As	[Alt]+[F], [A]
Open existing document		Click File, then click Open	[Ctrl]+[O]
Undo most recent action		Click Edit, then click Undo	[Ctrl]+[Z]
Bold text		Click Format, then click Font; choose Bold, then click OK	[Ctrl]+[B]
Italicize text		Click Format, then click Font; choose Italic, then click OK	[Ctrl]+[I]
Underline text		Click Format, then click Font; choose Underline, then click OK	[Ctrl]+[U]
Align text left		Click Format, then click Paragraph	[Ctrl]+[L]
Align text right		Click Format, then click Paragraph	[Ctrl]+[R]
Center text		Click Format, then click Paragraph	[Ctrl]+[E]
Justify text		Click Format, then click Paragraph	[Ctrl]+[J]
Select All		Click Edit, then click Select All	[Ctrl]+[A]
Print active document	(skips dialog box)	Click File, then click Print	[Ctrl]+[P]
Exit Word		Click File, then click Exit	[Alt]+[F4]

A. Identify Key Features

Name the items indicated by callouts in Figure 1-16.

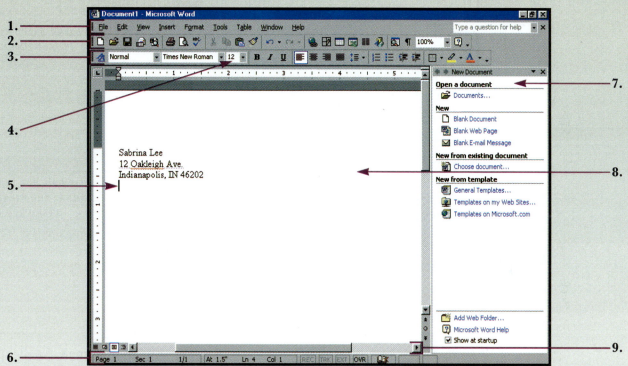

Figure 1-16 Elements of the Word screen

B. Select the Best Answer

10. The exact location where text appears when entered
11. The shape of characters such as letters and numbers
12. Reduces a window to a button on the Windows taskbar
13. The way in which text relates to the page's margins
14. A window that contains options for executing a command
15. Allows you to see how your document will appear when printed
16. The unit of measurement for font size
17. New feature that organizes numerous important features in one location

a. Alignment
b. Print Preview
c. Task Pane
d. Insertion point
e. Dialog box
f. Points
g. Minimize button
h. Font

quiz (continued)

C. Complete the Statement

18. In order to apply bold formatting to a section of existing text, you must first:
    a. Click one of the Formatting buttons
    b. Save the document
    c. Select the text to be formatted
    d. Click the Start button

19. Clicking the ![] button:
    a. Ejects the floppy disk
    b. Saves the active document
    c. Searches your hard drive for a file
    d. Selects the active line or paragraph

20. Clicking the ![] button on the Standard toolbar:
    a. Searches the document for spelling errors
    b. Magnifies the document
    c. Opens Print Preview mode
    d. Opens the Task Pane

21. The file extension for Word documents is:
    a. .txt
    b. .htm
    c. .doc
    d. .mp3

22. Examples of text formatting do not include:
    a. Font size
    b. Justification
    c. Text style
    d. File extensions

23. The icon that appears when Word recognizes text you have entered and can provide related commands is a:
    a. Shortcut
    b. ScreenTip
    c. SmartTag
    d. Task Pane

24. Text that is justified is:
    a. Grammatically correct
    b. Adjusted to meet both margins
    c. Bold
    d. Only visible in Print Preview

25. A button that turns a feature both on and off is called a:
    a. Drop-down list
    b. SmartTag
    c. Toggle button
    d. Scroll bar box

26. The Status bar provides all of the following information except:
    a. Number of misspelled words in the document
    b. Status of Overtype mode
    c. Number of pages in the document
    d. Position of the insertion point in the document

Build Your Skills

1. Identify a job that interests you and determine what the employer is looking for in a prospective employee:

   a. Go to the classified section of a newspaper or to a Web site that lists jobs and find a specific job listing that you think might suit you (Web sites you may try: www.careerbuilder.com, www.monster.com, www.jobs.com).

   b. Think about what skills and experience might be necessary to apply for the job you have found. Determine how your own skills and experience relate to the qualifications that the job would require.

2. Open Word and write a brief letter applying for the job (open the file wdskills1.doc to view a sample letter if you need some guidance in composing and organizing your letter):

   a. Launch Word using the Start menu.

   b. Following the model of wdskills1.doc, write your letter, beginning with the salutation and continuing with three or four short paragraphs, one each for your educational background, prior job experience, any other relative experience, and the reasons for your interest in this particular position.

   c. Include a closing, a few blank lines for a signature, and, finally, your name.

3. Format the text of the letter:

   a. Change the font size of the text to 11 pt.

   b. Change the font used in the letter to Garamond.

   c. Align the date with the right margin.

4. Print, save, and close the letter, and then exit Word:

   a. Use Print Preview to examine your letter and make any content or formatting changes you think are necessary.

   b. Close Print Preview and print one copy of your letter.

   c. Save the letter in your Word Files folder as Job Seek.doc.

   d. Close the document.

5. Open, edit, and save an existing document:

   a. Open Job Seek.doc from your Word Files folder.

   b. Align the date with the left margin so that it follows proper letter format.

   c. Save the changed document as a new file in your Word Files folder named Job Seek2.doc.

   d. Close the document and exit Word by clicking the application Close button on the right end of the Title bar.

interactivity (continued)

Problem Solving Exercises

1. Open a new document in Word and type your name, address, and today's date on consecutive lines. Then, skip a line and type a few sentences about an extracurricular activity or hobby that you enjoy. Format the document so that it matches the example shown in Figure 1-17. Finally, save the document in your Word Files folder as wdsolved1.doc and print it.

Figure 1-17 Problem solving exercise

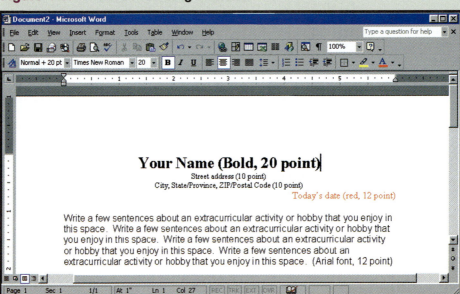

2. As the Assistant Technical Director at VER Recovery Corp., a collection agency, you have been asked to research various word processing programs to determine which is the best for your company's needs. After testing several products and considering prices, you have decided that the company would benefit most from adopting Microsoft Word 2002. Use a new blank Word document to write a memo to your boss that details this decision. Be sure to include your name as part of the document. When you are done, save the file in your Word Files folder as VER Recovery memo.doc.

3. Due to the quality of your work as Assistant Technical Director at VER, you have been promoted to Associate Technical Director. As your first act in your new capacity, you have proposed an expansion of the Information Technology department. Your proposal has been approved. Using Word, write a notice for the company bulletin board to announce the good news. Include a text in the document that calls for employees who are interested in transferring into the department to contact you (include your name). Take advantage of Word's formatting features such as bolding, underlining, font sizing, and text alignment to make your document lively. Save the document in your Word Files folder as VER IT notice.doc.

4. Your favorite entertainment-oriented Web site is looking for regular viewers who are interested in contributing movie reviews to the site on a weekly or monthly basis. If you are chosen based on your sample review, you will have your opinions published on the site on a regular basis and receive coupons for the site's online store. Use Word to write a review of the last movie you watched, either in a theater or at home. Use formatting techniques to call attention to the parts of your review that you feel are the most important, and therefore deserve emphasis. Save the document in your Word Files folder using the name Review by [Your Name].doc.

Editing Documents

Once you have entered text into a Word document, you may manipulate and edit the text to suit your needs. You can select text in a number of different ways so that you can modify portions of a document without affecting those parts of the document that do not require revision or updating. Word enables you to copy or move text, or delete it altogether.

In addition to the general blank document on which Word bases its standard new document, the program offers a multitude of other document types that can fulfill various needs. These templates serve as starting points for creating well-organized and effective documents such as letters, résumés, reports, Web pages, and so on. For even greater control over the appearance and functionality of a document template, Word provides features known as wizards. Wizards guide you through a series of steps in which you provide feedback as to what style of document you want to create and how the information in the document is presented.

You will find that the benefits of using Word are not limited to productivity features. Word places a great deal of importance on providing support for the user. For example, the program contains a powerful file search function that allows you to find documents you have saved based on a wide variety of search criteria. Word also includes a Help facility that is designed to help you access information about specific features and troubleshoot your work when you encounter problems. The Office Assistant is an animated character who acts as a liaison between you and the help files.

Lesson Goal:

Use various editing techniques to revise an existing cover letter, then create a résumé with a little assistance from Word.

- **Searching for Files**
- **Selecting Text and Undoing Actions**
- **Cutting, Copying, and Moving Text**
- **Copying and Moving Text with the Mouse**
- **Creating a Document with a Wizard**
- **Creating a Document with a Template**
- **Using the Office Assistant**
- **Other Word Help Features**

skill Searching for Files

concept

As you may have discovered, a single computer may contain a large number of locations in which you can store documents. It is not uncommon for users to need a document but not remember exactly where they saved it. Word's Open dialog box contains powerful search tools that you can use in this situation. The Search command is particularly helpful when you remember certain characteristics of a file such as a portion of its name, text it contains, or the date you last modified it.  If your Student Files for this book are stored on a floppy disk, make sure you have inserted the disk before beginning this Skill.

do it!

Use the Open dialog box to search for a file whose name you do not remember.

1. With Word running, click the Open button on the Standard toolbar. The Open dialog box appears.

2. Click the Tools button and then click Search on the menu that appears. The Search dialog box opens to the Basic tab. If it opens to the Advanced tab, click the Basic tab.

3. In the Search text box, type rice recipe.

4. Click the arrow on the right end of the Search in box in the Other Search Options section of tab. A list of locations will appear. If the check box next to My Computer does not contain a check mark, click the box to check it. Then click the drop-down arrow again to close the list.

5. Click the drop-down list box labeled Results should be to open a list of file types. Click the necessary check boxes so that only the one labeled Word Files contains a check mark. Then click the drop-down arrow to close the list.

6. Click the Search button. Word will begin searching all the drives on your computer for a Word file that contains the text "rice recipe." When the search is complete, you should see the file wddoit2-1.doc listed in the Results section (see Figure 2-1).

7. Double-click wddoit2-1.doc. The Search dialog box closes and the file is selected in the Open dialog box's File name box.

8. Click Open to open wddoit2-1.doc.

9. Close the file.

more

To be more specific about where you want to search for a file, click the "plus" sign next to My Computer on the Search in drop-down list. You then can select specific drives or folders to search in rather than all of your computer. Many of the top level locations can be expanded further for an even more precise search (see Figure 2-2). Narrowing down your search locations is especially helpful if the file you are seeking does not have any unique characteristics.

The Advanced tab in the Search dialog box contains a set of controls that permit you to set very specific criteria for a file search. If you open the Text or property drop-down list, as shown in Figure 2-3, you can select from a generous list of document details and file properties that are relevant to the desired file. You then select the condition under which that property occurs in the Condition drop-down list box. Finally, you enter the actual value of the search criteria in the Value text box. For example, you could instruct Word to search for files whose file names contain the word "report." Or you could search for files whose date of creation is between May 11, 2000 and October 21, 2001.

Figure 2-1 Search dialog box

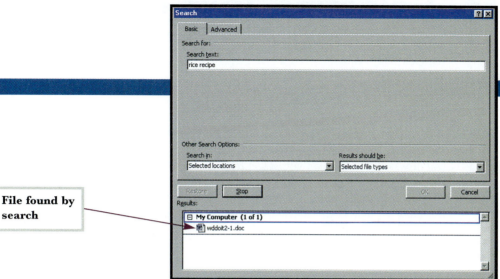

Figure 2-2 Selecting other search locations

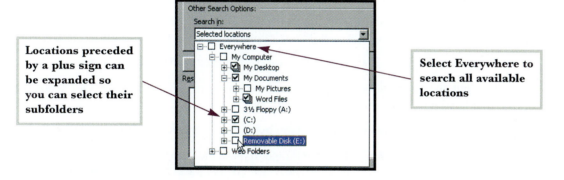

Figure 2-3 Advanced tab

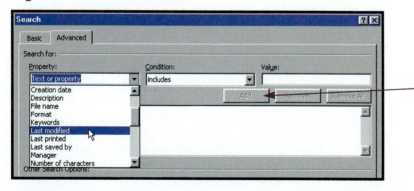

Practice

Search your computer for a Word file that contains the word sleuth. Open the file when you find it. Then save the file in your Word Files folder using the name mywdprac2-1.doc and close it. Remember, if your Student Files are stored on a floppy disk, the disk must be inserted in your floppy drive in order for you to complete this exercise.

skill Selecting Text and Undoing Actions

concept

Sections of existing text must be selected before you can modify them. Once you have selected a word, phrase, paragraph, or more, the selection acts a single unit that you can move, modify, or format. When you select text, it appears highlighted on the screen. That is, text that normally appears black on a white screen will be white on a black background. It is important to be careful when working with selected text as it is possible to erase an entire document by pressing a single key. You can use the Undo command, which reverses previous commands or actions, to correct such errors.

do it!

Practice methods of selecting text and undoing actions in a document.

1. Open the file wddoit2-2.doc.
2. Scroll down to the paragraph that begins My training experience ...
3. Select the paragraph by clicking just before the first letter, dragging the mouse pointer to the end of the paragraph, and then releasing the mouse button.
4. Type the letter X. The selected text will be replaced by the text you typed.
5. Click the Undo button on the Standard toolbar to reverse your previous action (typing X) and bring back the original paragraph.
6. Cancel the selection of the paragraph by clicking a blank area of the document.
7. Click at the beginning of the paragraph to place the insertion point in front of the first letter. Then hold down the [Shift] key and click at the end of the paragraph to select it.
8. Cancel the selection of the paragraph again.
9. Triple-click any portion of the same paragraph to select the whole thing again.
10. Close the file. You do not need to save any changes.

more

When clicking and dragging to select text, the selection will follow the mouse pointer letter by letter in the first word; subsequent words will be added to the selection one by one. If you drag down to the next line before reaching the end of the current line, the remainder of the current line and the portion of the next line up to the mouse pointer will be selected. To select a single line or multiple lines quickly, use the Selection bar, a column of space on the left edge of the document (see Figure 2-4). When the mouse pointer enters this area, it will appear reversed. Clicking in the Selection bar selects the entire line to the right of the pointer. Dragging up or down in the Selection bar selects the adjacent lines in the direction you are dragging. More ways to select text are shown in Tables 2-1 and 2-2. Keep in mind that [Num Lock] must be disabled in order to use the [Home], [End], and arrow keys on the numeric keypad.

The Undo command is an essential tool that easily corrects many of the worst mistakes you may make while using Word. The Undo and Redo buttons are grouped together on the Standard toolbar. Clicking the Undo drop-down list arrow opens a menu that allows you to undo multiple actions at once. The most recent action is listed first. If you want to undo an action that was not the most recent, you will have to undo all actions that followed it as well. The Redo command and its drop-down list work in a similar fashion, but instead reverse past Undo commands. After you perform many actions in Word, the Repeat command will become available on the Edit menu. You can use this command, or its keyboard shortcut [Ctrl]+[Y], to perform your last action again.

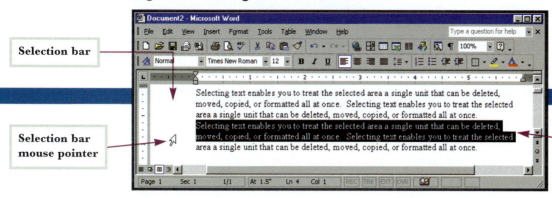

Figure 2-4 Using the Selection bar

- Selection bar
- Selection bar mouse pointer
- Selected text

Table 2-1 Selecting text with the mouse

Desired Selection	Action to take
A single word	Double-click the word
A sentence	Click the sentence while pressing [Ctrl]
A paragraph	Triple-click the paragraph or double-click next to it in the Selection bar
A line of text	Click next to it in the Selection bar
A vertical block of text	Click and drag while pressing [Alt]
The entire document	Triple-click in the Selection bar

Table 2-2 Selecting text with the keyboard

Desired Selection	Action to take
A single character	[Shift]+[←] or [Shift]+[→]
Word or portion of word to the left or right of insertion point	[Ctrl]+[Shift]+[←] or [Ctrl]+[Shift]+[→]
Paragraph or portion of paragraph above or below insertion point	[Ctrl]+[Shift]+[↑] or [Ctrl]+[Shift]+[↓]
To the beginning or end of a line	[Shift]+[Home] or [Shift]+[End]
To the beginning or end of a document	[Ctrl]+[Shift]+[Home] or [Ctrl]+[Shift]+[End]
A vertical block of text	[Ctrl]+[Shift]+[F8] (toggle on/off) and arrow keys
The entire document (Select All)	[Ctrl]+[A]

Practice

To practice selecting text and undoing actions, open the file wdprac2-2.doc and follow the instructions in the document. Close the file when you have completed the exercise. You do not need to save the document when you are done.

skill | Cutting, Copying, and Moving Text

concept

One of the greatest benefits of using a word processor like Word is that you can relocate existing text instead of having to type the entire document again. This saves you enormous amounts of time when you are revising your work. Within a matter of seconds, you can relocate entire paragraphs to a new place in the same document, or even in another document. Cutting and pasting text is one method of moving text. Copying and pasting text allows you to create a second instance of existing text while leaving the original text intact.

do it !

Move a paragraph in a letter using the cut-and-paste method.

1. Open wddoit2-3.doc and save it in your Word Files folder as Cutting and Copying.doc.
2. Select the paragraph that begins with This position … and the blank line below it, as shown in Figure 2-5.
3. Click the Cut button on the Standard toolbar. The selected text disappears.
4. Click after the period at the end of the first paragraph (the one that begins I am writing …) to place the insertion point there.
5. Click the Paste button on the Standard toolbar. The text you cut earlier, including the blank line, appears at the insertion point. The icon that appears when you paste is a Paste Options button. If you click the button, you can choose formatting options for the text you just pasted. These options include maintaining the formatting the text had at its previous location (the default option), acquiring the formatting in use at the new location, removing all formatting, and adding new formatting.
6. Press [Backspace] twice to delete the blank lines that have been added (as in Figure 2-6).
7. Click the Save button to save the changes you have made to Cutting and Copying.doc, and then close the document.

more

If you want to add existing text to another part of your document without moving the original text, click the Copy button, press [Ctrl]+[C], or select the Copy command from the Edit menu after you select the text, and then paste. Material that you cut or copy in Word is stored in a temporary storage area known as the Office Clipboard. The Cut command (and its keyboard shortcut [Ctrl]+[X]) removes material from the document and sends it to the Clipboard, while the Copy command simply sends a copy of what you selected there.

The Office Clipboard is capable of storing up to 24 unique pieces of data at once. When you execute the Paste command (its keyboard shortcut is [Ctrl]+[V]), Word pastes the data that arrived on the Clipboard most recently. If you want to paste a selection that was copied or cut earlier, open the Edit menu and click the Office Clipboard command. The Clipboard Task Pane will appear. Each item currently on the Clipboard, whether text, picture, or other, will be displayed in the pane. When you point to a particular item, a drop-down arrow will appear. Click this arrow to access commands that will let you either paste the item or delete it from the Clipboard (see Figure 2-7). No matter what method you use to paste, the data always appear wherever the insertion point is currently positioned in the document.

The Office Clipboard is common to all Office applications, so you may use it to share data among the different Office programs. In addition, the Windows operating system has its own Clipboard that can hold one item at a time. The last item you sent to the Office Clipboard also will be available on the Windows Clipboard, so you can share data from Office with non-Office programs. Clearing the Office Clipboard removes the contents of the Windows Clipboard as well. Both Clipboards are erased when you shut down your computer.

Figure 2-5 Selected paragraph to be moved

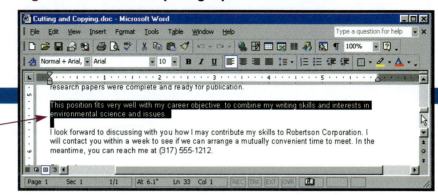

Selected text can be cut or copied

Figure 2-6 Letter after cutting and pasting paragraph

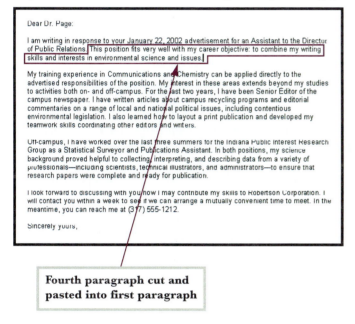

Fourth paragraph cut and pasted into first paragraph

Figure 2-7 Office Clipboard

Practice

To practice cutting, copying, and pasting text, open the Student File wdprac2-3.doc and follow the instructions given in the document. Save the document as mywdprac2-3.doc when you are done and close the file.

skill
Copying and Moving Text with the Mouse

concept

The drag-and-drop method of copying and moving text is quick and convenient for moving text a short distance within a Word document. In many instances, it is preferable to using the Cut, Copy, and Paste commands along with the Clipboard. Once highlighted, you can drag and drop any unit of text from a single character to multiple paragraphs.

do it!

Use the drag and drop method to move a paragraph in a letter.

1. Open the file wddoit2-4.doc.

2. Drag to select the second sentence in the first paragraph of the letter (This position … science and issues.).

3. Point to any portion of the selected text and press down the left mouse button. The mouse pointer will change to the drag-and-drop pointer, indicating that data—in this case text—are loaded and ready to be inserted. A dotted insertion point will also appear in the text. The dotted insertion point marks the point at which the text will be dropped when you release the mouse button.

4. Drag the mouse down and to the left until the dotted insertion point is to the left of the first letter in the second paragraph of the letter, as shown in Figure 2-8.

5. Release the mouse button. The selected text disappears from its previous location and reappears at the dotted insertion point.

6. Click a blank area of the document to cancel the selection of the text. The first two paragraphs of your letter should now look like Figure 2-9.

7. Save the document in your Word Files folder as Drag-and-Drop.doc and then close the file.

more

Dragging and dropping text moves it from its previous location, much like the Cut command. To copy text to another area by dragging while leaving the original text in its place, press and hold [Ctrl] on the keyboard before dropping the text. The drag-and-drop pointer will appear with a plus sign attached to it to signify that it will make a copy of the selected text. When you release the mouse button, the selected text will appear in its original location as well as at the insertion point (make sure you release the mouse button before you release the [Ctrl] key). The ability to drag and drop text is an editing option that you can turn on and off by going to the Edit tab of the Options dialog box, which you can access by clicking the Options command on the Tools menu.

If you are copying or moving text over a long distance in a document, it might be easier to use the Clipboard instead of the drag-and-drop method. It can be difficult to stop the scrolling of the screen accurately when you drag beyond the current screen.

Figure 2-8 Dragging and dropping text

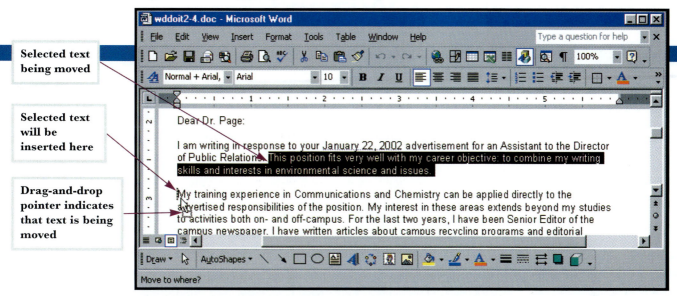

Figure 2-9 Letter after dragging and dropping

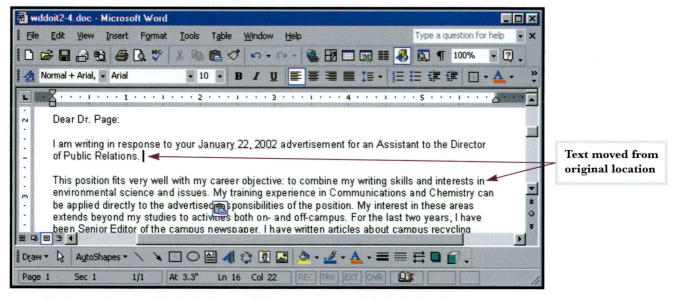

Practice

To practice moving and copying text with the mouse, open the Student File wdprac2-4.doc and follow the instructions given in the document. When you have completed the exercise, save the document as mywdprac2-4.doc and close the file.

skill  Creating a Document with a Wizard

concept

As you can probably imagine, Word is capable of producing very complex and stylized documents such as résumés, calendars, brochures, and Web pages. However, as a new user, you may not have enough confidence in your skills to begin designing one of these documents on your own. Or, you may be an experienced user who simply does not have the time it would require to design a professional-quality document from scratch. In both these cases, Word's document wizards can help you overcome your obstacles. A wizard is a series of dialog boxes that automates the document-creation process. The wizard guides you through the components of a document and asks you for the content that it needs to fill them.

do it !

Use a wizard to create a résumé for a student who is applying for a job.

1. If the Task Pane is not showing, click the New command on the File menu to display it. Click General Templates… in the New from template section of the New Document Task Pane. The Templates dialog box appears.

2. Click the Other Documents tab in the Templates dialog box to display the document templates and wizards it contains.

3. Click the Résumé Wizard icon to select it. A preview of the Résumé Wizard's typical output will appear on the right side of the dialog box (see Figure 2-10). Make sure the Document radio button is selected in the Create New section of the dialog box.

4. Click the OK button to launch the Résumé Wizard. The wizard begins at the Start step, which introduces the task at hand and provides an outline of all the steps to follow. The outline will be displayed throughout the wizard, with your current step marked by a green square, completed steps marked by dark gray squares, and incomplete steps marked by light gray squares. You can click these squares to jump to any step at any time.

5. Click the Next button to advance to the Style step.

6. Click the Elegant radio button to select this style of résumé, then click Next >.

7. For the Type step, click Next > to accept the default type, Entry-level résumé, and advance to the next step, Address. This step allows you to enter your name, address, phone and fax numbers, and e-mail address. Word automatically enters the name of the registered user in the Name text box and any other information that was provided during the software install procedure in the other boxes.

8. Type Sabrina Lee in the Name text box, 32 Oakleigh Ave. [Enter] Indianapolis, IN 46202 in the Address text box, and (317) 555-1212 in the Phone text box. Your text boxes should resemble those shown in Figure 2-11. Press [Tab] to move from one text box to another and select the extraneous information if there is any.

9. Click Next > to advance to the Standard Headings step. Once there, click the Interests and activities check box to add the heading to the résumé with the three default headings, Objective, Education, and Work Experience (see Figure 2-12). If any of those headings are not checked, click their check boxes. If any of the other headings are checked, click their boxes to remove the check marks.

10. Click Next > to advance to the Additional Headings step. No additional headings will be used in this résumé, so click Next > to advance again.

(continued on WD 2.12)

Figure 2-10 Templates dialog box

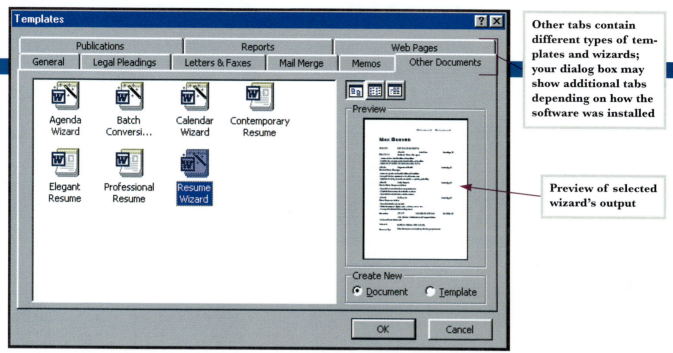

Figure 2-11 Résumé address

Figure 2-12 Résumé headings

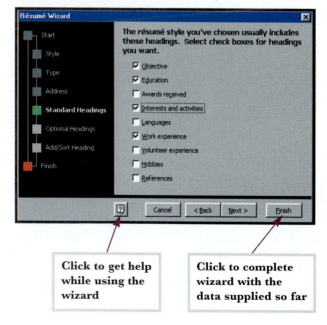

skill: Creating a Document with a Wizard (continued)

do it!

11. The Add/Sort Heading step allows you to insert a heading that was not included in the wizard, delete a heading that you had added previously, or change the order in which your selected headings will appear. Click Work Experience to select it, and then click the Move Up button [Move Up] to place Work Experience before Interests and activities. Click [Next >].

12. Click the Finish button [Finish]. Word constructs the résumé and displays it in Print Layout View. If the Office Assistant appears asking if you want to do more with the résumé, click the Cancel button [Cancel].

13. Under the Objective heading in the résumé, you will see a placeholder for the Objective text: [Type Objective Here]. Click this placeholder to select it, as shown in Figure 2-13.

14. Type To secure a position in communications or research in the field of environmental sciences as the objective.

15. Select the [Dates Attended] placeholder under the Education heading and type 1998-2002.

16. Select the [Company/Institution Name] placeholder on the same line and type Indianapolis University.

17. Select the [City, State] placeholder on the same line and type Indianapolis, IN.

18. Select the [Degree/Major] placeholder and type Bachelor of Science, Chemistry.

19. Select the placeholder preceded by a bullet at the bottom of the Education section and press [Backspace] three times to delete the placeholder, the bullet, and the blank line.

20. Use Figure 2-14 as a guide to completing the rest of the résumé. Replace Sabrina's name with your own name before continuing.

21. View the résumé in Print Preview and then print a copy of the document.

22. Save the document in your Word Files folder using the suggested file name Resume Wizard.doc, and then close the file.

more

The résumé you just created was left somewhat brief due to the constraints of this particular medium and method of instruction. In comparison, a résumé you might actually submit to a potential employer probably would be fleshed out more. For an entry-level résumé such as this one, you could include academic honors and awards that you have received. You also might add a section for course work you have completed that is related to the particular position for which you are applying. A heading under which you list the particular skills you possess, such as knowledge of specific software programs, computer languages, or foreign languages, can help illustrate the quality of your candidacy for a position. If you have any published works, you might want to list those as well.

The Résumé Wizard adds the information you supply to an existing document template. You may have noticed that the Other Documents tab in the Templates dialog box contains an Elegant Résumé template. You could use this template to produce the same document you created above without working through the steps of the wizard. You will learn how to create a document precisely in this manner in the next Skill. Some wizards and templates shown in the Templates dialog box are not included in the Typical install of Word or Office. Their icons serve as shortcuts that will prompt you to install the files from your CD-ROM before you can use them.

Figure 2-13 Selecting placeholder text

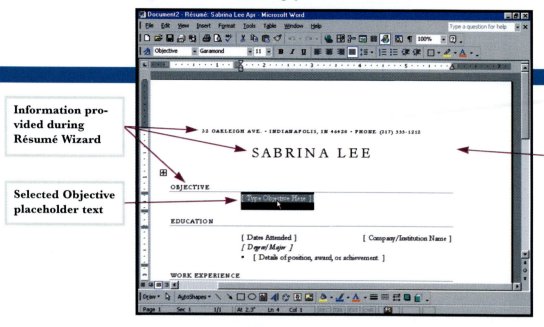

Figure 2-14 Completed résumé

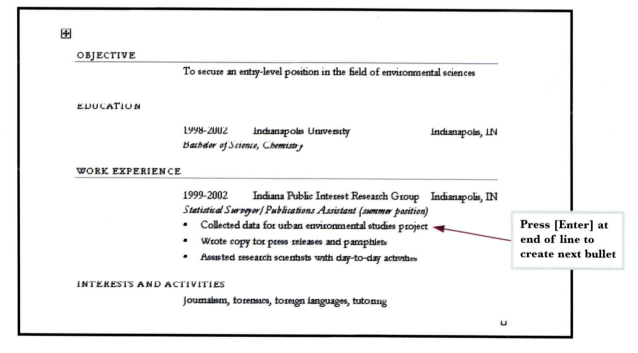

Practice

Use the Résumé Wizard to create a résumé for yourself. Select the Contemporary style résumé and the Entry-level type. The résumé should contain at least five Standard Headings and one Additional Heading. Once the document is set up, replace the placeholder text with the appropriate information about yourself. If you need to add more than one entry below a heading, you can do so by copying and pasting a previous entry and then editing it accordingly. When you are done, print the résumé. Then save it as mywdprac2-5.doc and close it.

LESSON TWO Editing Documents

 ## Creating a Document with a Template

concept

When you open a new document, its existing formatting and layout are based on a collection of stored settings. Together, these settings are known as a template. Word provides templates in many categories, including letters, faxes, memos, and Web pages; and styles, such as contemporary, professional, and elegant. When you open Word, the new document that appears is based on the Blank Document template, also known as the Normal template. Some of the settings associated with the Normal template are a blank page, the Times New Roman font, and a 12-point font size. Other templates already include text and graphics that you can customize to fit your needs. Templates serve as a great launching pad for creating documents that seem too complicated to begin from scratch. They can also help ensure consistency in documents.

do it!

Use a template to create an interoffice memo.

1. Click General Templates… in the New from template section of the New Document Task Pane. The Templates dialog box appears. If the Task Pane is not showing, click the New command on the File menu to display it.

2. Click the Memos tab in the Templates dialog box to display the document templates and wizards it contains, as shown in Figure 2-15.

3. Double-click the Professional Memo icon on the Memos tab. The dialog box closes and Word opens a memo immediately. If you would prefer to see a preview of the template before you create it, click the icon once to select it, and then open it.

4. The insertion point should already be in the first text placeholder, so you can begin entering your own information. Type 31 Smith Street [Enter] Indianapolis, IN 46202 [Enter] (317) 555-1313, as shown in Figure 2-16.

5. Click and drag over the placeholder text that says Company Name Here to select it, and then type Robertson Corp. to replace it.

6. Moving down the page, click the placeholder text [Click here and type name] in the To: field, and then type All Employees.

7. Click the placeholder text in the From: field and type Eduardo Alfonso, HR Director.

8. Click the placeholder text in the CC: (Courtesy Copy) field and type Anna Hayes, President.

9. The Date: field already should be filled in with today's date. Click the placeholder text in the Re: field and type Payroll Dates. The upper portion of the memo should now look like Figure 2-17.

(continued on WD 2.16)

Figure 2-15 Memos tab

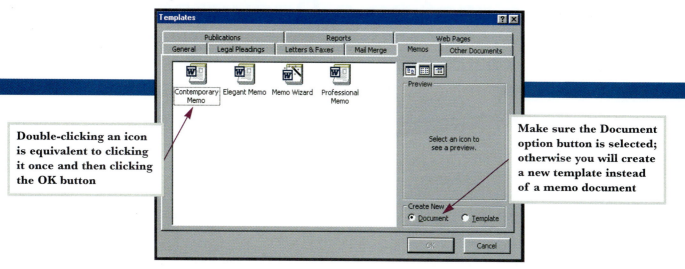

Double-clicking an icon is equivalent to clicking it once and then clicking the OK button

Make sure the Document option button is selected; otherwise you will create a new template instead of a memo document

Figure 2-16 Adding text to a template document

Figure 2-17 Completed upper portion of memo

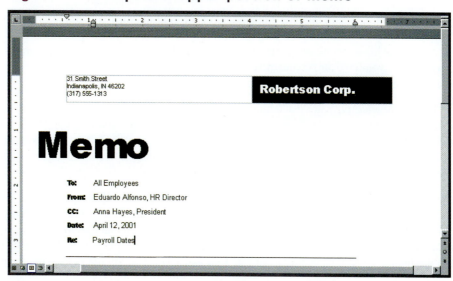

Creating a Document with a Template (continued)

10. Scroll down until you can see the portion of the memo below the horizontal line that divides the top of the memo from the bottom. The text you see is a brief guide to using the template.

11. Select the first line of the instructional text, How to Use This Memo Template, down to the end of the paragraph below it. All of the instructional text should now be selected (see Figure 2-18) and will be deleted as soon as you start typing your own text.

12. Type the following text:

    As many of you know, our budget for the next fiscal year was recently approved. The new budget has necessitated a change in the way we run our payroll. From now on, the payroll will be run strictly on the 1st and 15th of every month instead of every two weeks regardless of date, as was done previously. We hope that this change does not present too many inconveniences for you. If you have concerns about the new policy, please feel free to see me in person. [Enter]

    Your memo should now look like Figure 2-19. Add your name below the memo text.

13. View your memo in Print Preview and then print a copy of it.

14. Save the memo in your Word Files folder as Payroll Memo.doc, and then close the file.

more

Templates vary in the type and amount of information they contain. Some look like finished documents because they contain placeholders that tell you where to insert specific kinds of information. Others merely provide instructions on how to use the template in order to create the various elements needed in the document. And wizards, as you have already learned, automate part of the document-creation process by asking you to provide information that is then incorporated into the template.

Realize that the elements of a template are just a guide. You can accept them or reject them as you see fit. For example, suppose you are writing a memo like the one above, but you have no need for the courtesy copy line. You simply could select that line of text and delete it from the document. On the other hand, suppose you are using a résumé template and want to add more than one job under the Work Experience heading. All you have to do is copy and paste the existing placeholders in that section to make a duplicate set of them.

It is also important to understand how a template works from a file perspective. When you open a template, it immediately produces a fresh document file based on the template's settings. Therefore, you are not actually working in the template file. It has simply generated the document in which you are working. If you make useful changes to the elements of a document that originated from a template, you do have the ability to save that document as a template itself. That way, you can produce new documents from it in the future. To do this, select Document Template (*.dot) as the file type in the Save As dialog box.

Figure 2-18 Replacing the template's instructional text

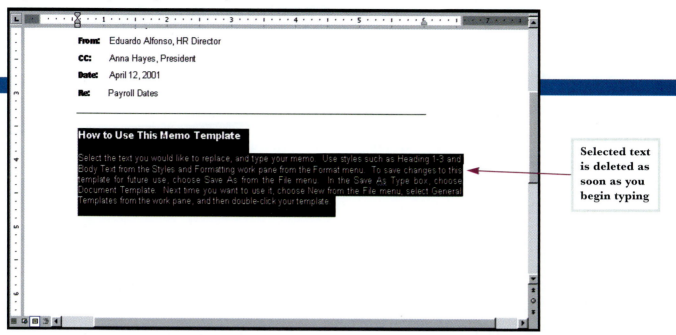

Figure 2-19 Completed memo

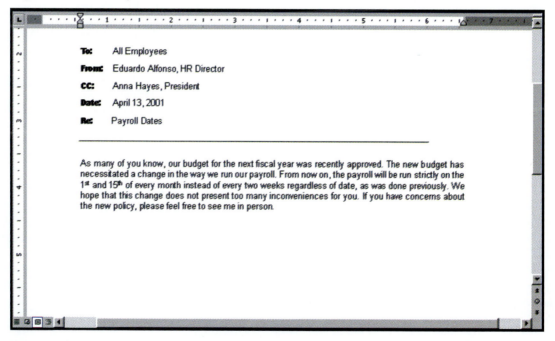

Practice

Use the Elegant Memo template to write a memo from yourself to Eduardo Alfonso, Human Resources Director, commending him and thanking him for his good work. Print a copy of the finished memo and save it as mywdprac2-6.doc. Then close the file.

skill Using the Office Assistant

concept

Word offers a number of built-in help features that you can use when you encounter problems or just have a question about a particular aspect of the program. One of these features is the Office Assistant, an animated character who provides several methods for getting help in Word. When activated, the Assistant will provide tips related to your current activity. The Assistant also will sense when you are trying to complete a particular task and offer to guide you through it, or you can ask the Assistant a question.

do it!

Ask the Office Assistant about Smart Tags.

1. Click Help on the Menu bar, then click Show the Office Assistant. The Office Assistant will appear on your screen.

2. Click the Office Assistant to open its dialog balloon, and then type How do I use Smart Tags? as shown in Figure 2-20.

3. Click the Search button [Search]. The Assistant searches Word's Help files for answers to your question and presents a list of topics.

4. Click the topic named Use smart tags, as shown in Figure 2-21. A Help window containing the topic you selected appears alongside the Word window (see Figure 2-22).

5. Read the Help file, and then click its Close button [X] to remove it from the screen.  Notice that the Ask a Question drop-down list box [How do I use smart tags?] on the Menu bar now contains the question you asked the Office Assistant. This gives you quick access to the Help topic in case you want to consult it again.

6. Click Help on the Menu bar, then click Hide the Office Assistant. The Assistant disappears from the screen.

more

Each question you ask the Office Assistant during a Word session is added to the Ask a Question drop-down list. To access the questions you have asked previously, click the arrow at the right end of the Ask a Question drop-down list box. When you click a question on this list, the list of Help topics found earlier by the Office Assistant will appear. You then can click the topic of your choice. If you want to ask a new question without using the Office Assistant, click inside the Ask a Question box itself, type your new question, and press [Enter] on the keyboard. The Ask a Question drop-down list is erased when you exit Word.

When the Office Assistant is showing and has a tip for you, a lightbulb icon will appear above the Assistant. Click the lightbulb to receive the tip.

Once you have hidden the Assistant several times, you will be asked if you would prefer to turn off the feature instead of just hiding it. The option of turning off the Assistant is also available in the Options dialog box, which you can access by clicking the Options button [Options] in the Assistant's dialog balloon. The Options tab in the Office Assistant dialog box, shown in Figure 2-23, also allows you to control how the Assistant behaves and what kinds of help it provides. The Gallery tab contains animated characters that you may use as your Office Assistant in place of the default paper clip character. While previews of the other Office Assistant characters are available on the Gallery tab, you must install the characters from your Word 2002 or Office XP CD-ROM in order to use them.

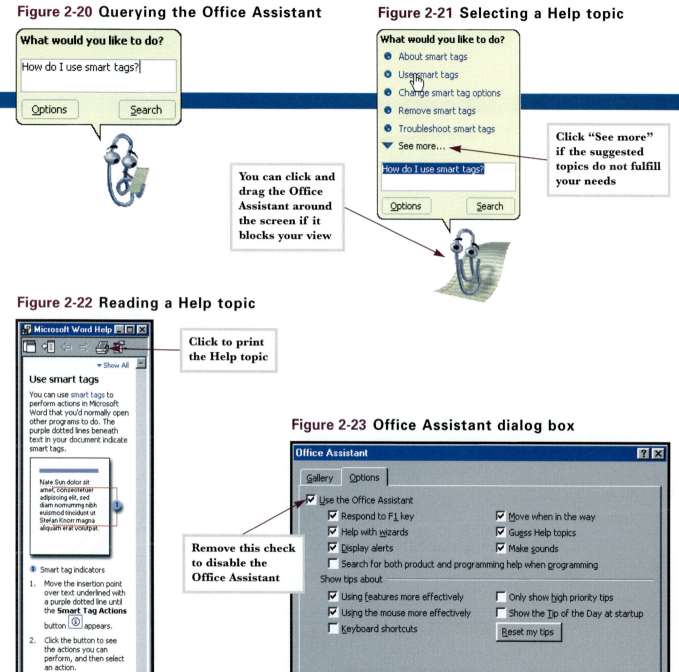

Figure 2-20 Querying the Office Assistant

Figure 2-21 Selecting a Help topic

Figure 2-22 Reading a Help topic

Figure 2-23 Office Assistant dialog box

Practice

Use the Office Assistant to read Help files on the following topics: new features in Word, ScreenTips, and checking spelling in a document. If you have a printer available, print any one of the Help files that you find. Close the Help window, and then turn off the Office Assistant as described in the More section and as depicted in Figure 2-23 above.

skill

Other Word Help Features

concept

For those that would prefer to obtain help without making use of the Office Assistant, Word offers a number of alternatives. As you have seen, ScreenTips help you identify elements of the Word window such as toolbar buttons. The What's This? command extends the power of ScreenTips to include feature names and descriptions of their functions. Perhaps most important of all, all of Word's Help files are available to you in an extensive Microsoft Word Help facility that does not require the participation of the Office Assistant. If you have not turned off the Office Assistant as instructed on the previous page, do so now.

do it!

Use the What's This? command and the Help feature to improve your knowledge of Word.

1. With a blank document open, click Help on the Menu bar, and then click What's This? on the Help menu. The mouse pointer now appears with a question mark attached to it.

2. Click the Show/Hide button ¶ on the Standard toolbar with the What's This? pointer. A ScreenTip appears explaining the function of the button you just clicked (see Figure 2-24). If you click document text with the What's This? pointer, the Reveal Formatting Task Pane will appear. This Task Pane summarizes the formatting in use on the selected text.

3. Click the mouse again to erase the ScreenTip.

4. Click the Microsoft Word Help button on the Standard toolbar. The Microsoft Word Help window opens alongside the application window with links to particular areas of help and a list of commonly requested Help topics.

5. Click the Show button at the top of the Help window. The window expands so that you can see the Help tabs. The Answer Wizard tab functions just like the Office Assistant, allowing you to ask a question and receive a list of suggested Help topics.

6. Click the Index tab, which allows you to search an alphabetical list of keywords.

7. Begin to type Web page in the text box labeled 1. Type keywords. Before you finish typing, the scrolling list box below will have scrolled to match what you have typed.

8. Click the Search button to find Help topics related to the selected keyword. The found topics will be listed in the box labeled 3. Choose a topic (see Figure 2-25). The first topic will be selected and the text of its related Help file will be displayed on the right side of the window.

9. Click the Help topic titled Create a Web page. Its Help file now appears to the right. In this case, it is a list of subtopics. Click the subtopic titled Create a Web page based on a template for detailed instructions on how to complete the task (see Figure 2-26).

10. Click the Close button in the Help window to close the Microsoft Word Help facility.

more

The Help facility's Contents tab is organized like an outline or the table of contents you might find in a book. It begins with a main level of broad topics symbolized by book icons, each of which can be expanded to reveal more specific subtopics. You can click these subtopics on the Contents tab to display their related Help files on the right side of the window, just as on the Index tab. When the window is expanded, the Show button changes to a Hide button in case you want to collapse the window into single panel again.

Figure 2-24 What's This? ScreenTip

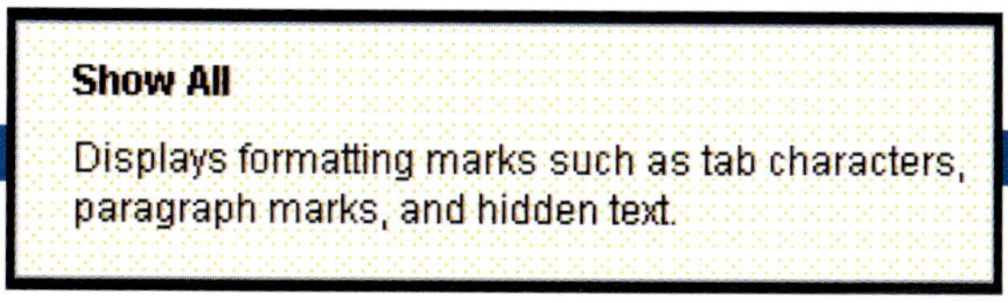

Figure 2-25 Help topics found by keyword

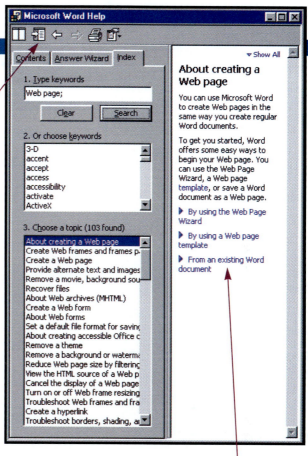

Figure 2-26 Viewing a subtopic

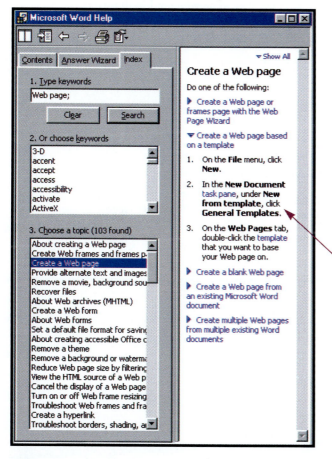

Practice

Open the Microsoft Word Help facility and use the Index tab to find Help topics related to the keyword format. Then read the Help files for the topics named Reveal formatting and Remove formatting from text. Close the Help window when you are done. Finally, use the What's This? command to get help on the Paste button.

shortcuts

Function	Button/Mouse	Menu	Keyboard
Search for a file from Open dialog box	Tools ▼, then click Search		
Search for a file from Task Pane	🔍	Click File, then click Search	
Undo last action	↶	Click Edit, then click Undo [action]	[Ctrl]+[Z]
Redo last undone action	↷	Click Edit, then click Redo [action]	[Ctrl]+[Y]
Repeat last action		Click Edit, then click Repeat [action]	[Ctrl]+[Y]
Cut selection to the Clipboard	✂	Click Edit, then click Cut	[Ctrl]+[X]
Copy selection to the Clipboard	📋	Click Edit, then click Copy	[Ctrl]+[C]
Paste newest item on Clipboard	📋	Click Edit, then click Paste	[Ctrl]+[V]
Get help	❓	Click Help, then click Show the Office Assistant or Microsoft Word Help	[F1]
Get a detailed ScreenTip for a screen item		Click Help, then click What's This?	[Shift]+[F1], then click the item
Show/hide nonprinting characters	¶		[Ctrl]+[*]

quiz

A. Identify Key Features

Name the items indicated by callouts in Figures 2-27 and 2-28.

Figure 2-27 Editing tools

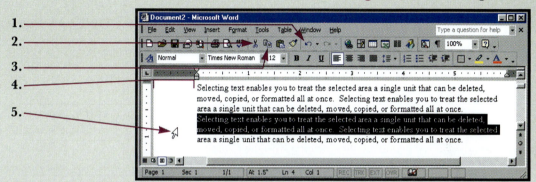

1.
2.
3.
4.
5.

Figure 2-28 More editing tools

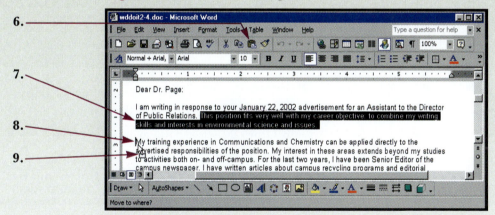

6.
7.
8.
9.

B. Select the Best Answer

10. Allows you to reverse several recent actions at once
11. Offers suggestions about using Word effectively and answers your questions
12. A series of dialog boxes that automates the creation of a document
13. Action that enables you to select an entire paragraph
14. A temporary storage area for cut and copied data
15. One of Word's Help tabs
16. A preformatted document with instructions and/or placeholder text
17. Button that appears when you insert data from the Clipboard

a. Index
b. Triple-click
c. Undo drop-down list
d. Paste Options
e. Template
f. Wizard
g. Clipboard
h. Office Assistant

quiz (continued)

C. Complete the Statement

18. When you start Word, the program opens with a document whose formatting and layout are based on the:

    a. Last document used

    b. Active buttons on the Formatting toolbar

    c. Blank Document template

    d. Résumé template

19. To copy selected text to another location with the mouse:

    a. Drag and drop the selected text

    b. Double-click the desired location

    c. Erase the Clipboard

    d. Drag and drop the selected text while pressing [Ctrl]

20. A wizard differs from a template in that:

    a. A wizard contains no graphic items

    b. A wizard uses information provided by you

    c. Documents created with templates cannot be edited

    d. A wizard can be used only once

21. To select the text from the insertion point to the end of the line:

    a. Click the paragraph mark

    b. Press [Ctrl]+[Home]

    c. Click next to the line in the Selection bar

    d. Press [Shift]+[End]

22. Double-clicking in the Selection bar:

    a. Opens the Templates dialog box

    b. Selects the entire document

    c. Selects the adjacent paragraph

    d. Minimizes the document window

23. You can revisit the Help topics produced by previous questions to the Office Assistant by using the:

    a. Ask a Question drop-down list box

    b. Search dialog box

    c. Contents tab

    d. What's This? command

24. You know the What's This? command is active when:

    a. The mouse pointer includes a plus sign

    b. The mouse pointer points to the right

    c. The mouse pointer includes a question mark

    d. The Help tabs are visible

25. Clicking the Paste button:

    a. Inserts the last item sent to the Clipboard

    b. Copies the selected text to the Clipboard

    c. Clears the Clipboard

    d. Opens the Clipboard Task Pane

26. You can use the Search dialog box to locate a file if you know:

    a. Part of the file name

    b. The date the document was created

    c. Text that appears in the document

    d. All of the above

interactivity

Build Your Skills

1. Search for a file and open it:

    a. Open the Search dialog box (from the Open dialog box) or the Basic Search Task Pane (click).

    b. Search for a Word file on your computer that contains the text Diana Voorhies.

    c. Open the file and save it in your Word Files folder as Monahan.doc.

2. Select and delete portions of the document:

    a. Select the last sentence of the second paragraph (He was really great …) by clicking it while pressing [Ctrl].

    b. Delete the selected sentence.

    c. Select the postscript near the end of the document by triple-clicking it.

    d. Add the text that follows the postscript to the end of the document to the selection by pressing [Ctrl]+[Shift]+[End].

    e. Delete the selected text.

3. Select and move paragraphs in the document:

    a. Select the third paragraph (the one that begins On a slightly …) by double-clicking next to it in the Selection bar.

    b. Drag the selected paragraph to the blank line following the next paragraph and drop it there.

    c. Select the first paragraph (Thank you very much …) by triple-clicking it.

    d. Cut the selected paragraph to the Clipboard.

    e. Paste the paragraph you just cut after the final paragraph of the document, before the name of the writer.

    d. Save the changes you have made to the document and close it.

4. Create a document using a wizard:

    a. Open the Templates dialog box and run the Memo Wizard.

    b. Create a Contemporary style memo with the title Word 2002 Memo.

    c. Address the memo to your instructor or administrator. Do not include a CC: field.

    d. Select the other options as you wish.

    e. When you finish the wizard, add text to the memo informing the addressee how you have created the document.

    f. View the document in Print Preview and then print a copy of the memo.

    g. Save the file in your Word Files folder as Word 2002 Memo.doc.

    h. Close the file.

interactivity (continued)

Build Your Skills (continued)

5. Create a document using a template:

   a. Use the Templates dialog box to open a document with the Contemporary Fax template.

   b. Fill out the fax cover sheet with the following information:
   Address: 12345 Laloma Blvd., Coral Bay, FL 01000
   To: Sir or Madam   Fax: (860) 555-6412
   From: [Your Name]   Date: [Today's Date]
   Re: Reservation   Pages: 1
   CC: Happy Travels, Inc.
   For Review

   c. Type a sentence or two in the lower half of the document explaining that you are confirming a hotel reservation.

   d. Save the document as Fax Cover Sheet.doc and close it.

6. Use Word's Help facilities:

   a. Ask the Office Assistant What are some useful keyboard shortcuts?

   b. Choose the Help topic called Keyboard shortcuts and read one of the subtopics under it.

   c. Show the Help tabs if they are not already visible in the Microsoft Word Help window.

   d. Search for topics related to the keyword view.

   e. Read each of the subtopics found under the topic About ways to view a Word document.

   f. Close the Help window and turn off the Office Assistant.

Problem Solving Exercises

1. You are about to graduate from college with a Fine Arts degree in Photojournalism. Your ambition is to find a job that will one day allow you to travel around the world taking evocative photos for a major magazine or newspaper. Since you are just starting out, you know that you may have to settle for a position with slightly less freedom for now. Use the Professional Résumé template to construct an Entry-level résumé that you can send to local newspapers and less-established magazines in search of a photojournalist position. However, do not sell yourself short. Emphasize your talents and experience as an amateur photojournalist and do not lose sight of your long-term goals. Customize the document as necessary—moving, adding, and deleting headings as necessary. When the résumé is done, print it and save it in your Word Files folder as Photo Résumé.doc.

2. As the owner and CEO of a rapidly expanding financial consulting firm, you are very proud to have had your best recruiting season ever. You have hired six outstanding recent college graduates from this year's recruiting class. Use the Letter Wizard to write a letter of congratulations to the head of your recruiting department. Select the Contemporary Letter design and the Full Block style. Preview and print the letter, then save it as Congrats Letter.doc.

Problem Solving Exercises (continued)

3. While at a talent showcase for local bands in Ithaca, NY, you have seen an act that looks more promising than any other that you have seen in your career as a talent scout. Since you brought along your laptop, you have decided to fax your boss at National Talent right away to tell her about the band you have seen. Use the Elegant Fax template to create a fax cover sheet. Since the template includes a section in which you can add the message you want to send, the fax may consist of only this one sheet. Complete the cover sheet, including your discovery at the showcase. Preview the finished document with Print Preview, and save it as New Talent Fax.doc.

4. The résumé depicted below was originally created with the Résumé Wizard using the Contemporary style and the Functional type. The document has since been edited and formatted to some degree. Use the skills you have learned so far in Word to recreate the document to the best of your ability, substituting your own name and address. Print the document and save it as Liaison Résumé.doc.

Figure 2-29 Résumé example

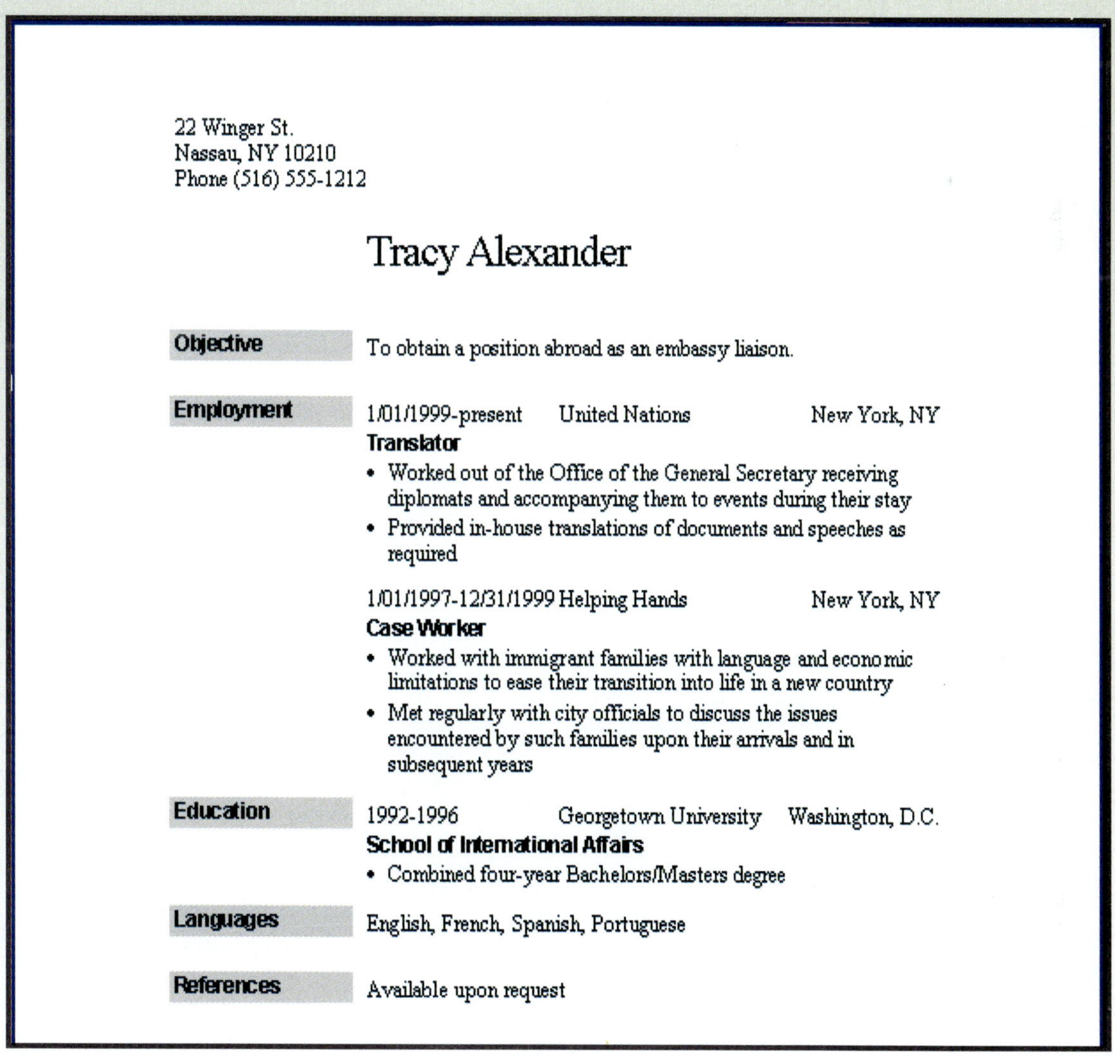

22 Winger St.
Nassau, NY 10210
Phone (516) 555-1212

Tracy Alexander

Objective To obtain a position abroad as an embassy liaison.

Employment 1/01/1999-present   United Nations   New York, NY
Translator
- Worked out of the Office of the General Secretary receiving diplomats and accompanying them to events during their stay
- Provided in-house translations of documents and speeches as required

1/01/1997-12/31/1999 Helping Hands   New York, NY
Case Worker
- Worked with immigrant families with language and economic limitations to ease their transition into life in a new country
- Met regularly with city officials to discuss the issues encountered by such families upon their arrivals and in subsequent years

Education 1992-1996   Georgetown University   Washington, D.C.
School of International Affairs
- Combined four-year Bachelors/Masters degree

Languages English, French, Spanish, Portuguese

References Available upon request

Advanced Editing

- Setting Up a Page
- Inserting Page Numbers
- Inserting Footnotes and Endnotes
- Applying Paragraph Indents
- Changing Line Spacing
- Inserting Page Breaks
- Working with Multiple Documents
- Using the Format Painter
- Checking Spelling and Grammar
- Using AutoCorrect
- Inserting Frequently Used Text
- Using the Word Thesaurus
- Finding and Replacing Text

Word allows you to add many different types of formatting to a document. There are three types of formatting: text-level formatting, paragraph-level formatting, and document-level formatting.

Text-level formatting, which was covered in Lesson 1, refers to all formatting that applies to individual characters in a document—such as font style, font size, and options such as bold and italics. No matter where text appears, these characteristics can be applied to single letters or entire sections of text.

Paragraph-level formatting covers the characteristics that can be applied to a paragraph or group of paragraphs. These features include alignment, indents, line spacing, line numbering, and other aspects that cannot be applied to a single character.

Document-level formatting includes options such as page margins or options called headers or footers. Headers, which appear at the top—or head—of a page, often contain document titles. Footers, which appear at the bottom—or foot—of the page, often contain page numbers.

Once a document has been typed and formatted to meet your needs, Word offers several proofreading aids to assure the quality of the finished document. For example, Word has a spelling checker that spots misspelled words throughout the document. Word also has a feature called AutoCorrect that can actually fix common typing and spelling mistakes automatically, as they are made. Additionally, Word contains a built-in thesaurus—or synonym finder—that makes it easier for you to find a word with the precise meaning needed for a particular context. Finally, if you decide to change a word or phrase that occurs in several places, especially in longer documents, Word can search your document for all instances of the item and replace it with a different word or phrase that you prefer.

Lesson Goal:

Add advanced formats to individual documents and learn how to use time-saving formatting commands. Learn how to proofread documents and make changes using correction tools.

Setting Up a Page

concept

Word gives you control over many aspects of formatting at the document level. These include margins, gutters (the space between two columns of text or the space formed by the inner margins of two facing pages), page orientation, paper sizes, section divisions, headers and footers, and vertical alignment of text on a page. Changing document-level formatting enables you to control how a document appears on both your screen and on a printout.

do it!

Reduce the left and right margins of a research paper.

1. Open Student File wddoit3-1.doc and save it in your Word Files folder as Report1.doc.
2. Click File, then Page Setup. The Page Setup dialog box appears.
3. If necessary, click the Margins tab to bring it to the front of the dialog box for viewing (see Figure 3-1).
4. Click the downward-pointing arrow at the right end of the Left box three times to reduce Word's default margin setting from 1.25 inches to 1 inch. The Preview area on the right side of the dialog box reflects your change to the left margin.
5. Triple-click the Right box to select it. Type the number 1 to replace the selected value of 1.25. Since inches is the default setting for measurements in Word, you do not need to add the quotations marks that represent that measurement.
6. Click OK to apply the changes to the document and to close the dialog box. The text of your document now may extend beyond the edges of your screen. If so, solve this viewing problem by reducing the Zoom percentage on the Standard toolbar so you can see to the edges of the page (see Figure 3-2).
7. After changing the left and right margins, save and close the document.

more

The Page Setup dialog box for Word 2002 differs somewhat from the corresponding box in previous versions of Word. Word 2002's dialog box now has three tabs—Margins, Paper, and Layout—instead of four. A few command options have been added, and some previously existing options have moved to different tabs to accommodate the simpler tab arrangement. The Margins tab enables you to adjust top and bottom document margins, as well as the left and right margins you altered in the Skill above. This tab also enables you to adjust the width and location of a gutter (the extra space at the edge of a page reserved for binding documents) and to change page orientation. The Page tab allows you to adjust page size to the type of paper in your printer, to pull paper from a different paper source in the printer, and to alter other print options as your printer's features permit. The Layout tab contains options to adjust document sections, header and footer options, the vertical alignment of text and/or graphics on a page, and line numbering and border options.

Figure 3-1 Page Setup dialog box

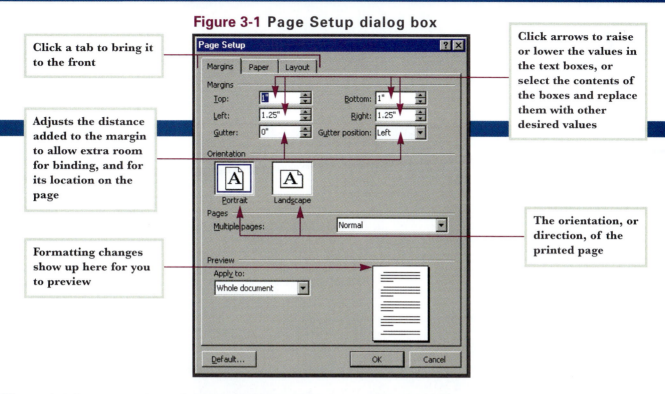

Figure 3-2 Report1.doc after setting 1" left and right margins

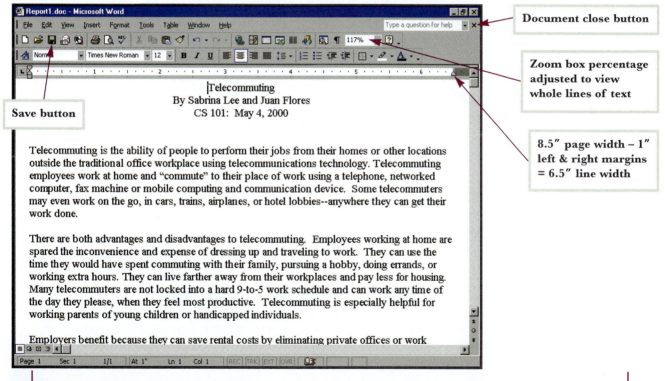

Practice

Open the Student File wdprac3-1.doc and save it in your Word Files folder as mywdprac3-1.doc. Practice adjusting page margins using the Page Setup dialog box under the File menu. When you have completed the practice exercise, resave and close mywdprac3-1.doc with your changes.

LESSON THREE **Advanced Editing**

 **Inserting Page Numbers**

concept

Word can insert page numbers into documents at different locations and in various styles. Word inserts numbers automatically so you do not have to add a page number to each page individually. You also can add a prefix to each page number to identify chapters or sections, or choose to leave off the number of the first page of a document if that first page serves as a title page.

do it!

Add centered page numbers to the report and view them.

1. Open Student File wddoit3-2.doc and save it in your Word Files folder as Report2.doc.

2. Click Insert, then click Page Numbers to open the Page Number dialog box (see Figure 3-3).

3. Click the Alignment box, then click Center to change the horizontal position of each page number from the default right setting to center.

4. Click Format... to open the Page Number Format dialog box (see Figure 3-4).

5. Make sure the Page Number Format dialog box displays Arabic numerals (1, 2, 3...) instead of letters or Roman numerals. If it does not, click the box, then click 1,2,3... to select Arabic numerals.

6. Click OK to close the Page Number Format dialog box and return to the Page Numbers dialog box.

7. Click OK to confirm and apply the Arabic numeral formatting. Word automatically shifts to Print Layout View so you can see the page numbers. If you add pages to a document that already is formatted with page numbers, the numbers will update automatically.

8. Scroll to the bottom of the page to see the inserted page number (see Figure 3-5). Click to save the changes you have made to Report2.doc, and then close the document.

more

The numbers you've added to the document do not appear in Normal View. Recall, however, that Word allows three other major ways to view documents. You can access these three views in two ways. First, you can click the View menu and then select Web Layout View, Print Layout View, or Outline View. Second, you can move among these same three views, and in the same order, by using the View buttons at the left end of the horizontal scroll bar at the bottom of the Word window. The current view is indicated by a square white background (or, on some monitors, a soft blue background) around the selected view button. Web Layout View displays your document as it would appear if viewed with a Web browser. Print Layout View displays your document as it will appear when printed, including page numbers. This view retains the Ruler and the Standard and Formatting toolbars. Outline view enables you to use Word's outlining features to structure text with headings and subheadings. Additionally, Print Preview displays how your document will look when printed, without non-printing characters but with items not seen in the default Normal View, such as headers, footers, and page numbers. Unlike Print Layout view, Print Preview lacks the Standard and Formatting toolbars, but has a Print Preview toolbar and magnifying tool. Other view options include Header and Footer, which displays headers and footers in an editable text box, and Full Screen, which shows only the document window.

Figure 3-3 Page Numbers dialog box

Figure 3-4 Page Numbers Format dialog box

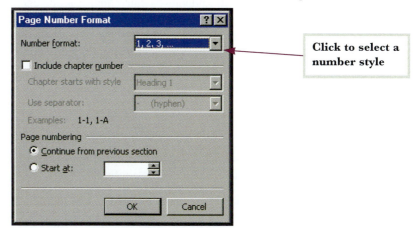

Figure 3-5 Report2.doc with page number

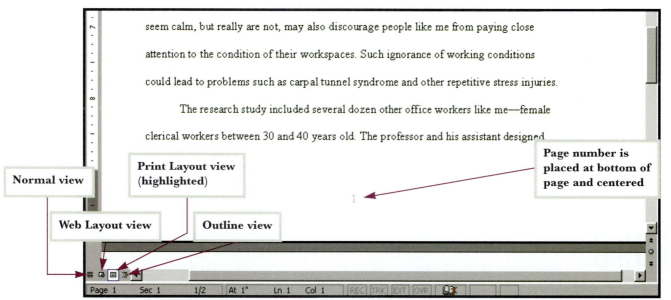

Practice

Open the Student File wdprac3-2.doc and save it in your Word Files folder as mywdprac3-2.doc. Follow the instructions at the beginning of the practice file to practice inserting page numbers using the Page Numbers dialog box under the Insert menu. When you have completed the practice exercise, resave and close mywdprac3-2.doc with your changes.

skill  Inserting Footnotes and Endnotes

concept

Footnotes and endnotes often appear in academic or longer business documents. Footnotes—which appear at the bottom, or "foot," of a page—often comment or expand upon the main text. Endnotes—which appear at the end of a document—usually provide references for further study. Both kinds of notes contain two parts—a note reference mark (usually a number elevated slightly—or superscripted—above the main line of text) and the note text. Word has a convenient feature that helps you automatically create, format, and number such notes.

do it!

Add a footnote at the end of a research paper and then view the new note.

1. Open Student File wddoit3-3.doc and save it in your Word Files folder as Report3.doc. Make sure that you are seeing the document in Normal view.

2. Position the insertion point at the end of the first paragraph, after the words can do work. This is where the note reference mark will appear.

3. Click Insert, click Reference, and then click Footnote. The Footnote and Endnote dialog box will appear with Footnote (the Word default setting) selected (see Figure 3-6).

4. Click Insert to insert the footnote using the current settings. Word inserts the note reference mark at the insertion point and opens a note pane at the bottom of the Normal view window (see Figure 3-7).

5. At the insertion point, type the following text: These "anytime, anywhere" work environments are sometimes called "virtual offices" because work can be performed outside of the traditional physical office setting and work schedule. Then click Close to leave the note pane and return to the document window.

6. Click View, then click Print Layout. Scroll to the bottom of the page and view the footnote in its proper place (see Figure 3-8). Alternately, position the mouse pointer over the note reference mark in the text so the footnote text will appear on your screen as a ScreenTip.

7. Save and close your document, Report3.doc, with the changes you have made.

more

In the Footnote and Endnote dialog box, the Continuous option in the Numbering area and Whole Document option in the Apply changes to box are more default settings not discussed above. With these options selected, Word automatically renumbers note reference marks throughout the whole document as you add or remove footnotes and/or endnotes, so there will be no break in their continuity. By clicking the Endnotes option in the Location area, you can place notes at the end of a document. By clicking the Number Format box in the Format area, you can change the numbering system from Arabic numerals to letters or Roman numbers. The Numbering box allows you to restart your chosen numbering system on a new page or new document section. And if you've divided your document into sections, the Apply changes to box enables you to make even more adjustments.

As Figure 3-7 shows, the note pane is a separate part of the Normal view screen for entering footnote (or endnote) text. You can access all footnotes (or endnotes) through the note pane. The default formatting for footnote text is 10-point Times New Roman, left aligned. You can change this formatting while in the note pane as you can with text in any other part of a document. In Normal view, double-clicking the note reference mark opens the note pane. In Print Layout view, double-clicking the note reference mark moves the insertion point to the related footnote.

Figure 3-6 Footnote and Endnote dialog box

Footnotes is default setting; click *Endnotes* to place notes at end of document

Adjusts placement of footnotes and endnotes on a page

Click here to change numbering system from Arabic numerals to letters, Roman numerals, etc.

Opens Symbol dialog box to insert custom marks such as asterisk, dagger, etc. instead of numbers, letters, etc.

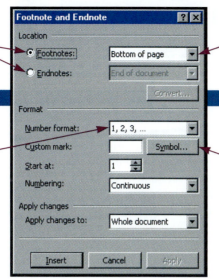

Figure 3-7 Note Pane with footnote text

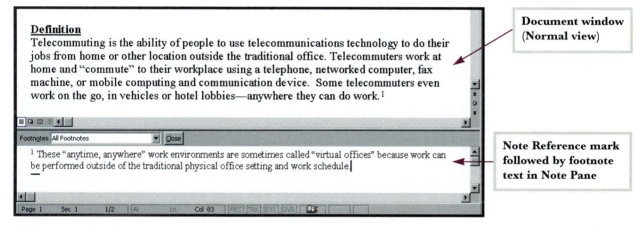

Document window (Normal view)

Note Reference mark followed by footnote text in Note Pane

Figure 3-8 Viewing a footnote at the bottom of a page

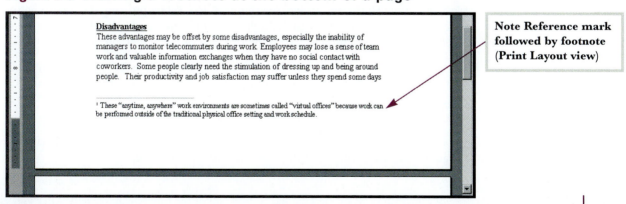

Note Reference mark followed by footnote (Print Layout view)

Practice

Open the Student File **wdprac3-3.doc** and save it in your Word Files folder as **mywdprac3-3.doc**. Practice inserting footnotes at the ends of sentences by using the **Footnote and Endnote** dialog box under the **Reference** command of the **Insert** menu. When you have completed the practice exercise, resave and close **mywdprac3-3.doc** with your changes.

skill Applying Paragraph Indents

concept

Indenting paragraphs helps to format documents so readers can follow your line of thought more easily. To indent paragraphs in Word, you can use the Tab key on the keyboard, the Paragraph command on the Format menu, the Increase Indent button on the Formatting toolbar, or three Indent Markers on the Horizontal Ruler. The Tab key and Increase Indent button provide less indenting flexibility, while the Paragraph command and Indent Markers provide more.

do it!

Use the four indenting tools to structure a document for easier reading.

1. Open Student File wddoit3-4.doc and save it in your Word Files folder as Report4.doc.

2. Place the insertion point immediately to the left of the first word in the second paragraph, Estimate. Press the Tab key on your keyboard once to indent the first line by half an inch to the right. Word's default new blank document has Tab Stops every half inch. In this case, however, each time you press the Tab key, you are setting the First Line indent of the paragraph another half inch to the right. You could click the Smart Tag button that has appeared to change this indent to a tab.

3. Place the insertion point just to the left of the first word in the third paragraph, Choose. Click Format, then click Paragraph to open the Paragraph dialog box (see Figure 3-9). Under Indentation, click the Special arrow and then click First line. Click OK to close the dialog box and indent the first line of the paragraph by half an inch.

4. Place the insertion point immediately to the left of the first word in the fourth paragraph, As. Click the Increase Indent button once on the Formatting toolbar to indent all lines of the paragraph one-half inch.

5. Click immediately to the left of the first word in the fifth paragraph, Stick. Click at the left end of the Horizontal Ruler (see Figure 3-10). While pressing the mouse button, drag the First Line indent marker to the right until it reaches the half inch mark on the ruler. Release the mouse button to indent the first line of the paragraph one half inch.

6. Click immediately to the left of the first word in the sixth paragraph, Remember. Click Format, and click Paragraph to open the Paragraph dialog box. In the Indentation area, click the Special box, and click the Hanging option. Click OK to close the dialog box and indent the second and following lines one half inch.

7. Look at the variously indented paragraphs of the document in Print Layout view (see Figure 3-11). Save and close Report4.doc with your changes.

more

You can set your own tab stops by clicking the bottom half of the ruler where desired. After you set the tabs, you can drag and position them along the ruler with the mouse pointer. To remove a tab stop, click and drag it below the ruler. It will vanish when you release the mouse button. Clicking the tab alignment selector at the left end of the ruler selects various tab alignments that you can apply. As seen in the steps above, the First Line indent marker controls indentation of just the first line of selected paragraphs, while the Hanging indent marker controls all lines in selected paragraphs except for the first line. Like the Increase and Decrease Indent buttons, the rectangle below the Hanging indent marker (i.e., the Left indent marker) controls all lines of selected paragraphs. Because you can move indent markers anywhere on the ruler, the Left indent marker has more flexibility than the buttons, which you can set only to predetermined tab settings. When you open a blank document, the default settings for the indent markers are even with the margins.

Word 2002

WD 3.9

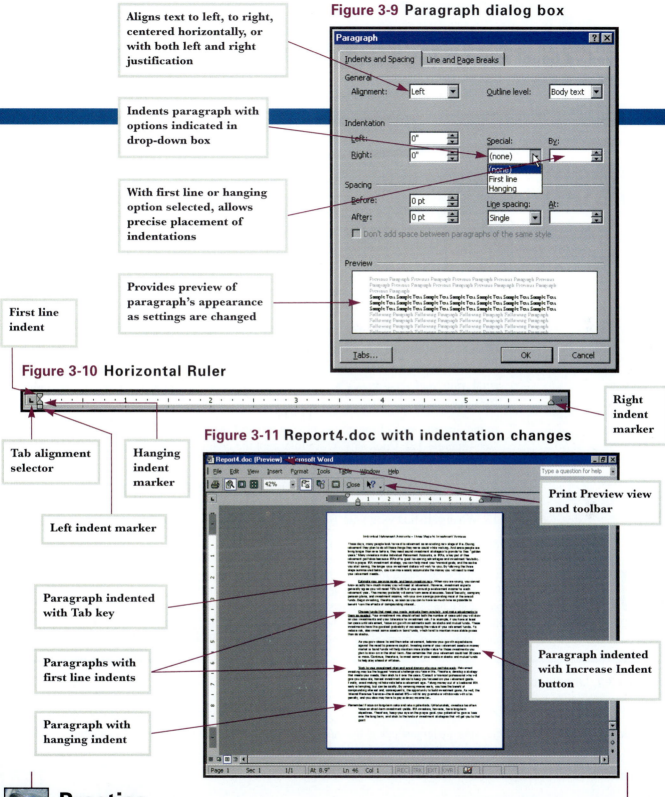

Figure 3-9 Paragraph dialog box

- Aligns text to left, to right, centered horizontally, or with both left and right justification
- Indents paragraph with options indicated in drop-down box
- With first line or hanging option selected, allows precise placement of indentations
- Provides preview of paragraph's appearance as settings are changed

Figure 3-10 Horizontal Ruler

- First line indent
- Tab alignment selector
- Hanging indent marker
- Left indent marker
- Right indent marker

Figure 3-11 Report4.doc with indentation changes

- Paragraph indented with Tab key
- Paragraphs with first line indents
- Paragraph with hanging indent
- Print Preview view and toolbar
- Paragraph indented with Increase Indent button

Practice

Open the Student File **wdprac3-4.doc** and save it in your Word Files folder as **mywdprac3-4.doc**. Follow the instructions of the paragraphs that appear in the file to practice indenting paragraphs using the **Paragraph** dialog box under the **Format** menu and using the **Horizontal Ruler** just below the **Formatting** toolbar. When you have completed the practice exercise, resave and close **mywdprac3-4.doc** with your changes.

skill  Changing Line Spacing

concept

The line spacing—or distance between adjacent lines of text—can be modified from the Paragraph dialog box. Word also allows users to change the spacing between paragraphs, without changing line spacing within those paragraphs. Many universities and businesses require written documents to conform to certain formatting standards, which often include spacing considerations. For example, professors generally require that research papers be double-spaced, while business supervisors require that all memos and letters be single-spaced.

do it!

Remove the spaces between paragraphs and double-space a report.

1. Open Student File wddoit3-5 and save it in your Word Files folder as Report5.doc. Be sure the document displays in Normal view. Delete each of the three blank lines between the four paragraphs of the main text by selecting the blank lines and pressing [Delete].

2. Click Edit, then click Select All to select the entire document. Click Format, then click Paragraph to open the Paragraph dialog box.

3. In the Spacing area of the dialog box, click the Line Spacing list box, then click Double (see Figure 3-12). Click OK to accept the changes you have made. Click anywhere in the document to remove the highlighting.

4. Click View, then click Print Layout. Scroll down in the document until you can see from the title to the first line of the second paragraph, and compare your results with Figure 3-13. When satisfied with your formatting results, return to Normal view.

5. Save and close the document, Report5.doc, with the changes you have made.

more

The Paragraph dialog box has a Preview box that shows you how the changes you are making will affect your text. The Word default setting is single spacing. If the spacing interval you want does not appear in the Line Spacing list box, the At box allows you to set spacing at any interval desired, such as 1.25 spacing or 0.9 spacing. The Before and After boxes control spacing before and after a selected paragraph. These boxes allow you to space individual paragraphs automatically at any interval without adding blank lines within any paragraphs in the document.

Table 3-1 Line Spacing

Option	Description
Single	Accommodates the largest font in that line, plus a small amount of extra space. The amount of extra space varies with the font being used.
1.5 lines	One-and-one-half times that of single spacing.
Double	Twice that of single spacing.
At least	The minimum amount of line spacing needed to fit the largest font or graphic on the line.
Exactly	A fixed amount of line spacing that Word does not adjust.
Multiple	Line spacing that increases or decreases by a percentage you specify. E.g., setting line spacing to 1.3 will increase the spacing by 30 percent over single spacing.

Figure 3-12 Paragraph dialog box with double spacing

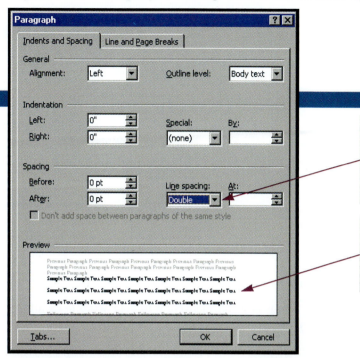

Double-spacing option selected. Other options include Single, 1.5 lines, At least, Exactly, and Multiple

Selection of double-spacing option creates appearance of double spacing in Preview box

Figure 3-13 Report5.doc, double-spaced

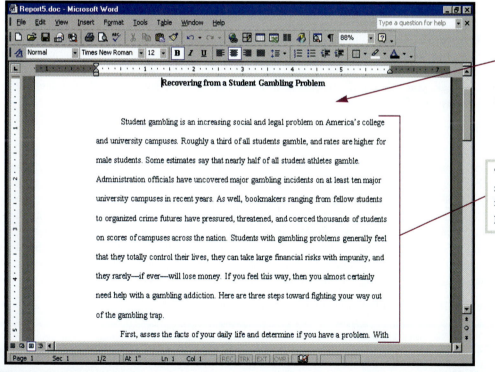

With double-spacing applied, the original double-spacing below the title becomes quadruple spacing.

The rest of the document is double-spaced, including between the paragraphs.

Practice

Open the Student File wdprac3-5.doc and save it in your Word Files folder as mywdprac3-5.doc. Follow the instructions of the paragraphs that appear in the file to practice line and paragraph spacing using the Paragraph dialog box under the Format menu. When you have completed the practice exercise, resave and close mywdprac3-5.doc with your changes.

skill Inserting Page Breaks

concept

When you fill a page in Word with text and/or graphics, the program inserts an automatic (or soft) page break and starts a new page with any additional typing or images you may have. To create a page break at a specific place in a document, you can insert a manual (or hard) page break. A manual break might be proper for a Works Cited page in a report, a new novel chapter, or a table or graphic that should stand out in a business document. Word also offers various section break options for dividing longer documents into subparts.

do it!

Place the References section of a report on a separate page.

1. Open Student File wddoit3-6 and save it in your Word Files folder as Report6.doc. Be sure you are viewing it in Normal view.

2. Place the insertion point before the word References at the head of the References section of the report. This word will become the first line of the new References page.

3. Click Insert, then click Break to open the Break dialog box. In the dialog box the Page Break option already is selected (see Figure 3-14).

4. Click [OK] to insert a page break at the insertion point. The References section will now appear at the top of a new page (see Figure 3-15). Word will automatically renumber the pages of the document to account for the new page. To remove a Hard page break, you would click next to it in the Selection bar to select it, and then delete it by pressing [Delete].

5. Save and close your document, Report6.doc, with the changes you have made.

more

In Normal view an automatic or soft page break looks like a dotted horizontal line. In Print Layout view it looks like a gap between two pages over a gray background. Earlier versions of Word could not eliminate the gray gap between the pages nor reduce the top and bottom margins to view more page area. Word 2002, however, has a new feature that performs those tasks. When in Print Layout, you simply place your insertion point over the gap. When you see the Hide White Space button, simply click it. The gap and margins will disappear, making it possible to view more page area. In the Section break types area, the Break dialog box also allows you to add Section breaks. A section is just a distinct part of your document that is separated from the rest. For example, as noted above, you could separate chapters in a book by using section breaks. Inserting a section break ends one section and dictates where the next will begin.

Consult Table 3-2 below for examples of types of section breaks that you can insert.

Table 3-2 Section Breaks

Option	Description
Next page	Inserts a section break and starts a new section on the next page.
Continuous	Inserts a section break and starts a new section on the same page.
Odd page	Inserts a section break and starts a new section on the next odd-numbered page.
Even page	Inserts a section break and starts a new section on the next even-numbered page.

Figure 3-14 Break dialog box

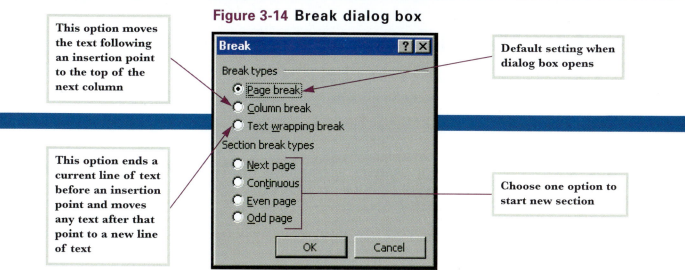

This option moves the text following an insertion point to the top of the next column

Default setting when dialog box opens

This option ends a current line of text before an insertion point and moves any text after that point to a new line of text

Choose one option to start new section

Figure 3-15 Report6.doc, after inserting manual (hard) page break

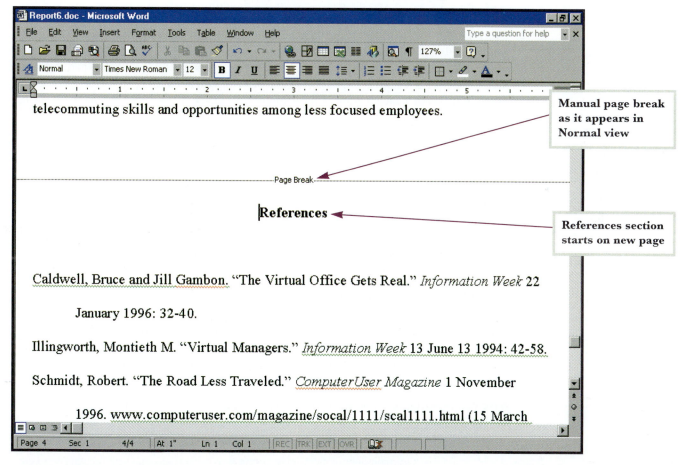

Manual page break as it appears in Normal view

References section starts on new page

Practice

Open the Student File *wdprac3-6.doc* and save it in your Word Files folder as *mywdprac3-6.doc*. Following the highlighted instructions that appear in the file, practice inserting various page and section breaks using the Break dialog box under the Insert command. When you have completed the practice exercise, resave and close *mywdprac3-6.doc* with your changes.

 **Working with Multiple Documents**

concept

Word, like many other programs, lets users work with more than one document at a time. You can create a new document or open an existing one without jeopardizing the active document. You can arrange document windows so you can see one, two, or more open documents simultaneously. You also can copy and move text between open documents using the Office Clipboard. This feature can save you from the time-consuming task of having to retype text that you want to use in another document.

do it!

Copy text created in one document and paste it into another document.

1. Open Student File wddoit3-7.doc and save it in your Word Files folder as Report7.doc. Keep the file open. Then open Student File wddoit3-7a.doc and save it in your Word Files folder as Report7a.doc. Report7.doc has a 6-inch text line, so its left and right margins are set at 1.25 inches. Report7a.doc has a 6.5-inch text line, so its left and right margins are set at 1 inch. (Ignore this difference, as the next few steps will adjust for it.)

2. Select all of the one paragraph in Report7a.doc, either by dragging over the paragraph or by triple-clicking anywhere inside it. While the paragraph is selected, click on the Standard toolbar or press the Copy command's keyboard shortcut, [Ctrl]+[C].

3. Click Window on the Menu bar, and then click Report7.doc to switch to that document. To switch to Report7.doc, you also could click its program button on the Windows taskbar at the bottom of your computer screen. If the taskbar is hidden, it is set in AutoHide mode. To make it appear, move your mouse pointer to the bottom of the screen.

4. With Report7.doc still open, click immediately after the period after the word tone at the end of the first paragraph. Press [Enter] twice to move the insertion point down two lines.

5. Click on the Standard toolbar to paste the copy of the paragraph from Report7a.doc. Scroll to the end of the inserted paragraph. Ignore the Smart Tag that appears near the last word of the inserted paragraph, king. If needed, adjust the blank spacing between the inserted paragraph and the one that begins with the word When so there is only one blank line between the paragraphs. Notice that the inserted paragraph from Report7a.doc now conforms to the 6-inch line of Report7.doc (see Figure 3-16).

6. Save and close Report7.doc with the inserted paragraph. Close Report7a.doc without saving any changes.

more

Word provides alternate ways to open documents (or other types of Word files) that you recently worked on. First, you can click the File menu and see the directory path and filenames of the four to nine documents opened most recently in Word on the computer. (To adjust the number of displayed filenames, you would click the Tools menu, click the Options command, click the General tab to bring it forward, enter the desired number of entries in the Recently used file list box, and then close the dialog box by clicking the OK button.) Second, you can click the Start button on the Windows taskbar and move your mouse pointer over the Document command. These two steps will display a list of just the filenames from any program opened most recently on the computer. Clicking one of these filenames will open the relevant file or make it the active document if it is already open. Remember that the active file is always the one in front, highlighted by a blue title bar. Inactive files will have a medium gray title bar (see Figure 3-17).

Figure 3-16 Report7.doc with pasted paragraph

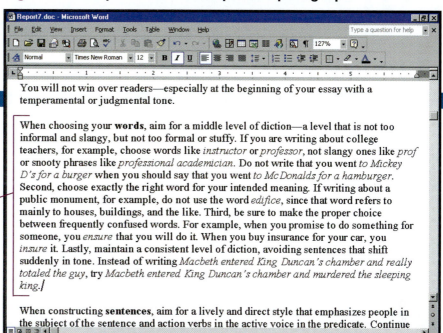

Paragraph copied from Report8.doc and pasted into Report7.doc

Figure 3-17 Active document "cascaded" on top of inactive ones

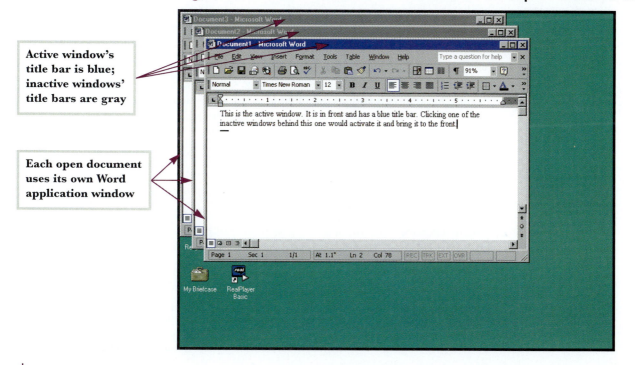

Active window's title bar is blue; inactive windows' title bars are gray

Each open document uses its own Word application window

Practice

Open Student File wdprac3-7.doc and save it in your Word Files folder as mywdprac3-7.doc. Then open Student File, wdprac3-7a.doc. Following the instructions in the two files, practice copying and pasting paragraphs from one document into another in the proper order. When you have completed the practice exercise, resave and close mywdprac3-7.doc with your changes. Close wdprac3-7a.doc with no changes.

skill: Using the Format Painter

concept

The Format Painter enables you to copy many formatting settings from selected text to another section of text. Whether you are working with just a word or a paragraph, Format Painter unifies document formatting without having to apply each formatting change separately. By reducing the need to format new text with repeated keystrokes or mouse clicks, this feature also saves you time. Format Painter is especially useful in documents like flyers and newsletters where distinctive formatting is common, even essential, to the document's appearance.

do it!

Use Format Painter to copy the formatting from one section of text to others.

1. Open Student File wddoit3-8.doc and save it as Report8.doc. Notice that the title is formatted as 12-point Arial Black, while the rest of the text is 11-point Arial Narrow.

2. Select the first question, Question—What is the Internet? Click the Font arrow and select Arial. Click the Font Size arrow and select 12. Click [B]; click [≡]. Click the arrow on the [▦▾] button, and click [▦] in the box that appears (see Figure 3-18). This action will apply a border around the line, margin to margin . With the first question still highlighted, click [🖌]. (The mouse pointer will change to a 🖌] when dragged onto the white document area.)

3. Move the insertion point to the left edge of your screen into the Selection bar so it changes to ⇗ . Place the mouse pointer at the same level as the second question, which begins Question—How does the Internet.... Click the mouse button. Notice that the formatting of the first question applies itself to the second.

4. With the second question still highlighted, click [🖌]. Move the insertion point into the Selection Bar so it again changes to a mouse pointer. Place the mouse pointer at the same level as the third question, and click the mouse. The formatting of the first and second questions applies itself to the third. Repeat this formatting process for the fourth question so all the questions are formatted alike.

5. Double-click the word Answer at the beginning of the first answer. Click [B], and then click [U]. This time, double-click [🖌].

6. With the Format Painter button highlighted, double-click the word Answer at the beginning of the second, third, and fourth answers. Notice that the formatting of the first word applies itself to the other three words. Click [🖌], or press [Esc], to deactivate Format Painter. Verify that your document now looks like Figure 3-19.

7. Save and close your document, Report8.doc, with the formatting changes.

more

As shown above, you click once on the Format Painter tool to copy a format to one other area but double-click to copy a format to multiple areas. After formatting those areas, remember to turn off Format Painter or you may format unintended spots. When formatting paragraphs, remember that the paragraph mark, ¶ , shows where you pressed [Enter] to go to a new line. Thus, to copy both text and paragraph formatting to another area, be sure to highlight the whole paragraph and its paragraph mark before activating Format Painter. To copy only text formatting, highlight the paragraph text and final period but stop short of the paragraph mark. (Display or hide the mark by clicking the Show/Hide button ¶ on the Standard toolbar.) Format Painter does have some limitations. It does copy formats such as font style, indents, line spacing, borders, etc. But it cannot convert, for example, plain text to WordArt or vice versa.

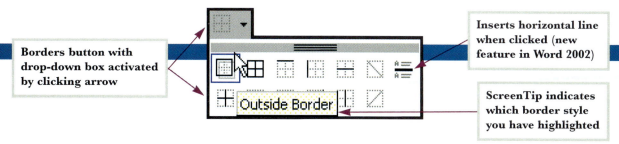

Figure 3-18 Outside border selected within Borders button

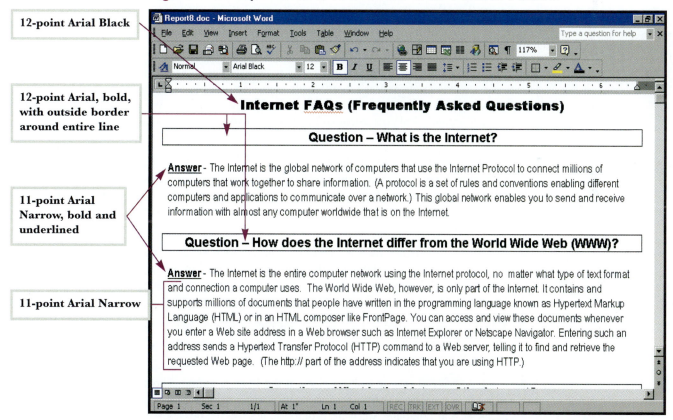

Figure 3-19 Report8.doc, formatted with Format Painter

Practice

Open Student File wdprac3-8.doc and save it in your Word Files folder as mywdprac3-8.doc. Following the instructions in the file, practice using Format Painter to copy formatting from one area of a document to another area. When you have completed the practice exercise the second time, resave and close mywdprac3-8.doc with the changes.

Checking Spelling and Grammar

concept

In default mode Word automatically checks a document's spelling and grammar. Basing decisions on a built-in dictionary and grammar checking program, Word then marks with wavy colored lines any words and phrases that Word does not recognize as correct. Using pop-up menus or the Spelling and Grammar feature on the Tools menu, you then can identify possible corrections to suspected errors and, if you desire, make appropriate changes. To complete this Skill, be sure the Check spelling as you type, Check grammar as you type, and Check grammar with spelling features are active in Word. To access these features, click the Tools menu, then the Options command, and then click the Spelling & Grammar tab to bring it to the front of the dialog box.

do it!

Check a document for spelling and grammar errors, and then correct them.

1. Open Student File wddoit3-9.doc and save it in your Word Files folder as Report9.doc. This is a sample paragraph with several spelling and grammar errors in it. Spelling errors (and correct spellings that Word's dictionary does not recognize) appear with a wavy red line under them. Grammatical errors appear with a wavy green line under them. So will grammatical constructions (such as passive verb forms) that are correct but that the grammar checker does not prefer.

2. Right-click the first word in the paragraph that is underlined with a wavy red line, processer. A pop-up menu appears with several suggested correct spellings. Move the mouse pointer over the first choice, processor (see Figure 3-20). To accept the correct spelling, click the mouse button. Word replaces the misspelled word with the selected correction.

3. Click Tools, then click Spelling and Grammar to open the Spelling and Grammar dialog box (see Figure 3-21). The next error will be highlighted in the upper area of the dialog box, and several suggestions for replacing it will appear in the Suggestions box in the lower area.

4. Select the correct word in the Suggestions box, grammar, and click [Change All] to correct all occurrences of this spelling mistake throughout the document. Word then highlights the accidentally repeated word in the phrase you you.

5. Click [Delete] that appears in place of the Change button. The second you disappears. Word now highlights the possessive form Word's. Since inanimate (non-living) items such as computer software usually do not use the possessive form, the grammar checker highlights this construction.

6. Click [Ignore Once] to ignore this unusual construction. Word now detects a grammatical error, noting that the plural verb provide does not agree in number with the singular subject it.

7. Click [Change] to change the highlighted word to provides, thereby creating grammatical agreement between the subject and verb and clarifying the meaning of the sentence. Next, the Spelling and Grammar checker highlights a proper name that it does not recognize.

(continued on WD 3.20)

Figure 3-20 Automatic spell checking in a pop-up window

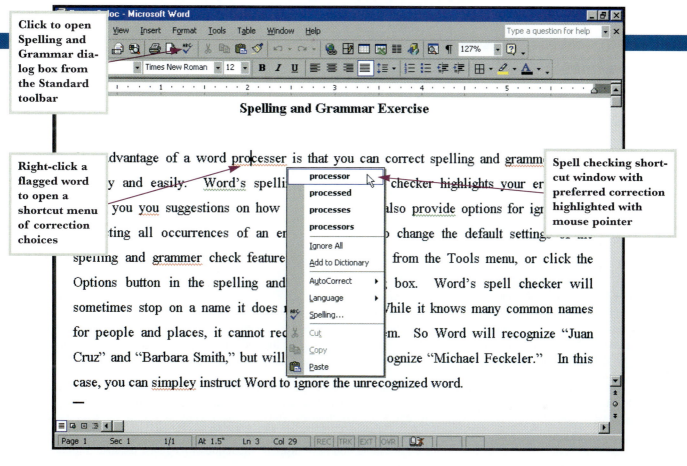

Figure 3-21 Spelling and Grammar dialog box

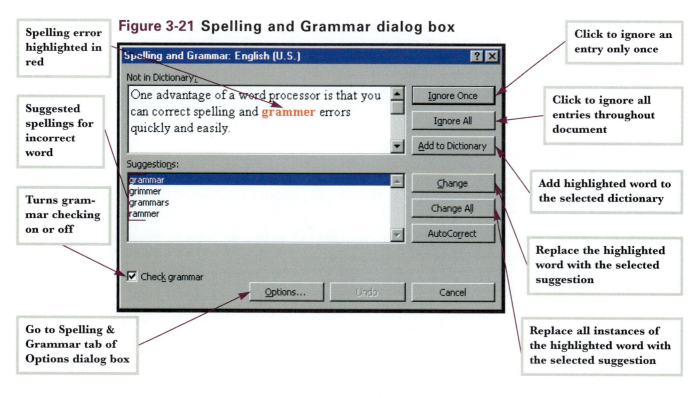

skill Checking Spelling and Grammar (continued)

8. Click [Ignore Once] to ignore the selected name, which is spelled correctly even though Word does not recognize it. Word now highlights the misspelled word, simpley.

9. Click [Change]. Word replaces simpley with the correct spelling, simply, and the Spelling and Grammar dialog box disappears. It is replaced with a small Microsoft Word message box notifying you that the spelling and grammar check is complete. To close the message box, click [OK].

10. Compare your corrected document with Figure 3-22. Correct any spelling or grammar errors that you may have missed.

11. Save and close your document, Report9.doc, with the corrections you have made.

more

As noted above, when the spelling checker comes across a word it does not recognize, it compares that word with similarly spelled words in its dictionary and marks it with a wavy red underline. These words are not based on an analysis of the sentence's meaning. Some words, even though spelled like the unrecognized word, will make no sense in the context of a corrected sentence. In the end, therefore, you must choose corrections carefully so they have not only the right spelling but also the correct meaning for your document.

The first section of the shortcut menu allowed you to select one word from a longer list of correctly spelled words resembling the word you clicked on. The second section allows you to ignore all instances of correctly spelled words (or to add correctly spelled words that you often use) that do not appear in Word's dictionary. The third section provides access to three features (a) AutoCorrect, which you will study in the next skill, (b) the Language dialog box, which permits use of dictionaries in over 200 languages or dialects other than American English (providing you have installed the required language pack) and (c) the Spelling dialog box. The fourth section allows you to cut, copy, and paste the right-clicked word.

Just as the Change All button in the Spelling and Grammar dialog box corrects all further instances of a selected word, so also the Ignore All button tells Word to skip all further instances. Word also takes capitalization into account when checking spelling. So if you told the program to ignore Interpenetrability, for example, it would still stop on interpenetrability if the lowercase form appeared in the document. Moreover, different copies of Word may recognize different words because users can add words permanently to Word's custom dictionary, a document that is unique to each copy of the program. Suppose, lastly, that the spell checker highlights a word it does not recognize but that you know is spelled correctly. By clicking [Add] in the Spelling and Grammar dialog box, you will add the word to the custom dictionary, which will not question the word again.

The grammar checker is a "natural language" tool and has the advantage that it identifies possible errors in the overall context of your document. But even a powerful word processing program such as Word has only so much computer code and operates on computers with finite amounts of power and memory. Therefore, the grammar checker cannot find all possible grammatical errors, only the most common ones.

To make Word more flexible, however, you can adjust some ways in which the program checks for errors. On the Spelling and Grammar tab of the Options command in Tools, for example, you can set preferences for which dictionaries to use, for checking words in all capital letters or words containing numbers, for checking Internet addresses, and for how formal a writing style you wish to enforce (see Figure 3-22).

Figure 3-22 Report9.doc, corrected version

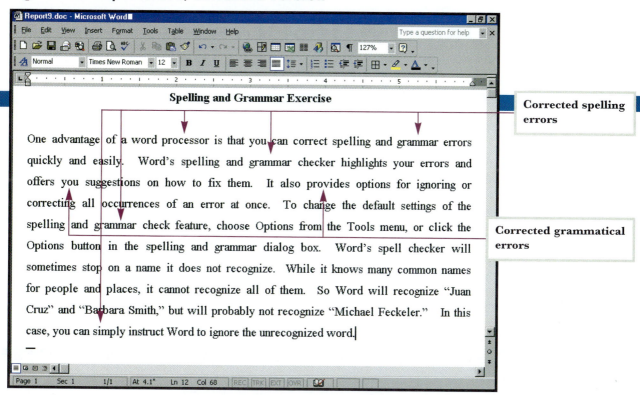

Figure 3-23 Spelling and Grammar tab of Options dialog box

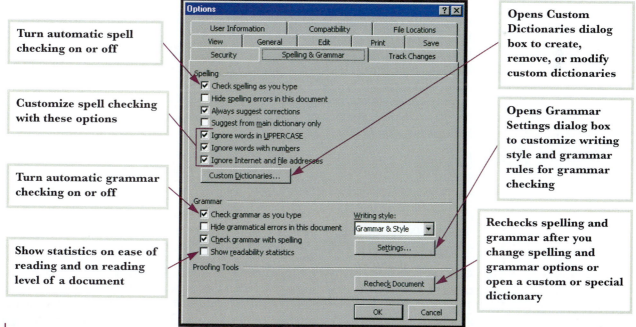

Practice

Open Student File wdprac3-9.doc and save it in your Word Files folder as mywdprac3-9.doc. Follow the instructions at the top of the first page to practice spell checking the report. Remember—Word sometimes marks words as errors because the Spell Check dictionary does not recognize them. Examine each marked item carefully before making a change. Resave and close the document, mywdprac3-9.doc, after the changes.

skill | Using AutoCorrect

concept

Word's AutoCorrect feature automatically detects and corrects frequently misspelled words, incorrect capitalizations, and other common typographic errors. For example, if you type abbout and then a space, the feature converts the misspelling to about. AutoCorrect converts certain characters and character combinations into symbols that represent them better (for example, (c) becomes ©). A new feature in Word 2002 even detects a misplaced letter, as in I like thi sfood. When you type a space after the second misspelled word, this feature will shift the incorrectly placed letter to its proper place to create the correct phrase, I like this food. AutoCorrect's default list of corrections includes many other fixes and enables you to add entries easily. The combined features of AutoCorrect help save users lots of retyping and, therefore, lots of time.

do it!

Set AutoCorrect to fix a common typing mistake and explore AutoCorrect's other features.

1. Open a new blank document by clicking 🗋 on the Standard toolbar.

2. Click Tools, and then click AutoCorrect Options. The AutoCorrect dialog box opens to the AutoCorrect tab. An insertion point appears in the Replace box.

3. In the Replace box, type the word corect, misspelling it intentionally. Press [Tab] to move the insertion point to the With box, and type the word correct (see Figure 3-24). To accept the change and close the dialog box, click [OK]. The blank document that you opened in Step 1 now should be in the active window. Word now will replace corect with correct in any document. However, if you cannot enter the misspelled and properly spelled words, determine if you are running Word 2002 from a network. If you are, the networked program may have security precautions preventing you from adding entries. If so, skip to Step 5.

4. Type the following sentence exactly as it appears: Word will now corect mistakes that i make. Notice that as you typed the sentence, Word fixed the misspelled word corect and automatically capitalized the personal pronoun i.

5. Press [Space] after the previous sentence, and then type the word many (lowercase, as shown) followed by a space. Word recognizes many as the first word of a new sentence because the word is preceded by a period and a space and, therefore, capitalizes it.

6. After the capitalized Many, type misc. mistakes are fixed automatically. Notice that although you typed a period and a space after misc., the word mistakes did not capitalize. This is because misc. is on AutoCorrect's Exceptions list along with most other common abbreviations. To see the list of exceptions, click Tools, click AutoCorrect Options, be sure the AutoCorrect tab is showing, and click [Exceptions...] to open the AutoCorrect Exceptions dialog box (see Figure 3-25).

(continued on WD 3.24)

Figure 3-24 AutoCorrect dialog box, with added cor-

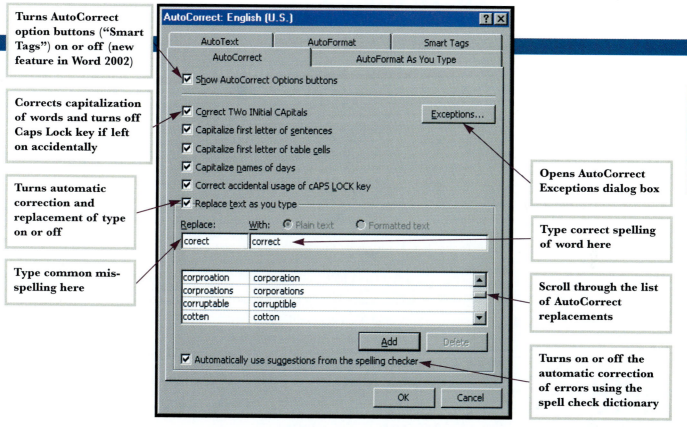

Figure 3-25 AutoCorrect Exceptions dia-

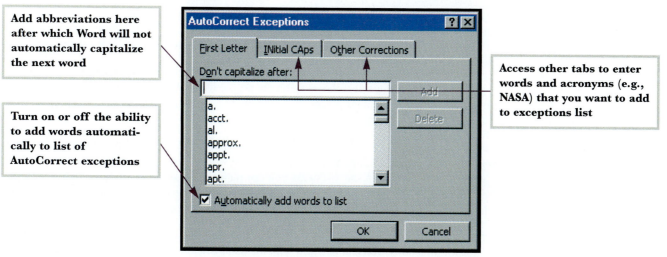

skill   Using AutoCorrect (continued)

do it!

7. Press [Space] after the previous sentence. Then type the following sentence exactly as it appears: Somem istakes are more obvious than others. Notice that as you typed the space after the letters istakes, Word shifted the misplaced letter m from the end of the word Some to the beginning of the group of letters. Press [Space] again.

8. Type the following sentence exactly as it appears: This is *bold* text, and this is _italic_ text. (In other words, type an asterisk [*] immediately before and after the word bold, and type an underscore [_] immediately before and after the word italic.) Notice that the word bold and the word italic change styles as you type. If these changes do not occur, click Tools, click AutoCorrect Options, and click the AutoFormat As You Type tab to bring it forward, if necessary. On this tab use a mouse click to place a check mark in the box for the option Bold and Italic with real formatting (see Figure 3-26). Close the dialog box by clicking [OK], and then retype the sentence.

9. Compare your corrected document with Figure 3-27, and then close the document. Unless directed otherwise by your instructor, do not save any changes.

more

The nine steps above expose you to several key tools in AutoCorrect, but this powerful and flexible feature can make many more types of corrections. For example, if you accidentally start a word with two capital letters, AutoCorrect will convert the second letter to lowercase. As part of its AutoFormat feature, AutoCorrect will convert the straight-styled quotation marks that were common on typewriters and early word processors (and which still can appear in Word 2002 to slightly curled marks (e.g., "La Tour Eiffel").

You can increase AutoCorrect's power and flexibility in at least three different ways. First, as you already know from Step 3 above, you can add your own common misspellings and related corrections on the AutoCorrect tab of the AutoCorrect dialog box. Second, as Figures 3-24 and 3-25 show, you can use the AutoCorrect Exceptions dialog box to add entries to its abbreviations list. Once you close the dialog box, Word will recognize the period and space after any new entries, and not capitalize the next word. (If you work in a field that uses many abbreviations, the Exceptions list will come in handy.) Third, on either AutoFormat tab in the AutoCorrect dialog box, you can turn on more correction features as your typing needs require.

If, on the other hand, you do not need all of the power that AutoCorrect provides, you can turn off some or all of its features. For example, to get rid of an entry that you do not want, select the entry on the proper list in the AutoCorrect dialog box and click [Delete]. If you are working in a computer lab or similar place where you share computers, do not delete any AutoCorrect entries that you did not add.

Smart Tags deserve special mention here because the Smart Tags tab appears in the AutoCorrect dialog box and these tags are a new feature in Word 2002 and other Office XP programs. Smart Tags are associated with various kinds of data but are not data themselves. Instead, these tags are a set of markers that appear with data you can manipulate. With Smart Tags enabled in your copy of Word, they will identify data with Smart Tag Indicators. A purple dotted line will appear under names, addresses, dates, and similar items. A small blue rectangle will appear under the beginning of Internet or e-mail addresses.

To use a Smart Tag, slide your insertion point over the indicator so a Smart Tag Actions button appears. As you click the button, a menu will appear with a list of tasks, or actions, you can perform with the data. Clicking on a name will enable you to use Microsoft Outlook to send mail, schedule meetings, and perform similar tasks. Clicking on an address will enable you to add it to your Outlook contacts, find the address on a map at www.expedia.com, and so on. The whole idea behind Smart Tags is to provide seamless, barrier-free interaction between the Office XP program you are using and many other programs, while reducing the need to move your mouse all over the screen. (For more information on Smart Tags, click [?], click the Contents tab, expand the purple Microsoft Word Help booklet, expand the Smart Tags booklet, and click on the desired topic.)

Figure 3-26 AutoFormat As You Type tab in AutoCorrect dialog box

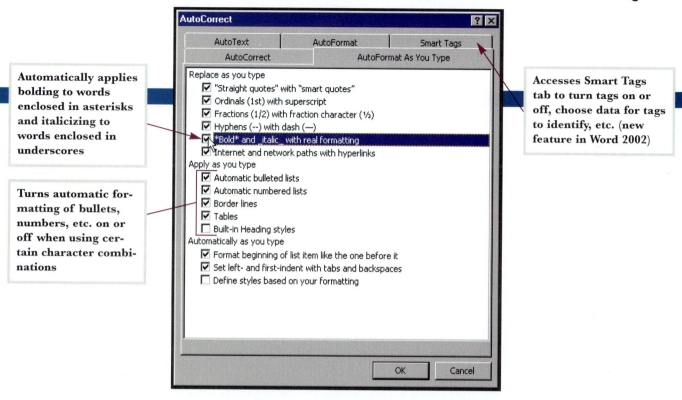

Figure 3-27 Opened document with AutoCorrections

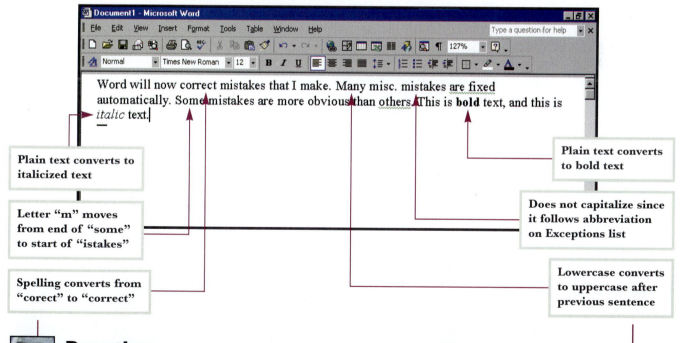

Practice

Open Student File wdprac3-10.doc and save it in your Word Files folder as mywdprac3-10.doc. Following the instructions at the beginning of the file, practice using Word's AutoCorrect feature. When finished typing, resave the file, mywdprac3-10.doc, and then close it.

skill: Inserting Frequently Used Text

concept

If you are like most people, you probably type a wide variety of documents for various subjects. However, you sometimes may have to type unusual, long, or complicated words or phrases over and over or use words that regularly appear in standard documents. When inserting frequently-used text in these latter situations, use Word's AutoCorrect feature to save time and effort. Also use the AutoText feature, which recognizes many words and phrases as you start typing them, predicts their outcomes in a ScreenTip, and then offers to complete them for you. For example, if you type Dear M, Word will suggest the AutoText Dear Mom and Dad. To accept the tip, press [Enter], and Word will insert the remaining text for you. If you do not want to accept the tip, or if the suggestion is incorrect, simply continue typing and the ScreenTip will disappear.

do it!

Use AutoCorrect and the AutoText features to insert frequently used text in a business letter.

1. Click [ ] to open a new blank document, and save it as Membership.doc.

2. Start typing today's date, starting with the day of the week, not the month. When you have typed the fourth letter of the day, a ScreenTip will appears that spells out the rest of the day. Press [Enter] to accept the completed spelling, and then type a comma. When the second ScreenTip appears to add the month, day, and year, press [Enter] to insert them. Press [Enter] twice again.

3. Type the inside address of the letter as follows:

   Mr. Joseph Kucharsky
   Walton Supermarkets
   7844 Industry Park Drive
   Middletown, NY 11007

4. Press [Enter] twice. Start typing the word certified. The ScreenTip for CERTIFIED MAIL will appear upon typing the letter t. When the ScreenTip appears, press [Enter] again to accept the completed text with its uppercase formatting. Press [Enter] twice.

5. Start typing the salutation of the letter, Dear Mr. Kucharsky and a colon. When you have typed Dear M, a ScreenTip will appear for Dear Mom and Dad. Do not stop typing, and do not backspace. Instead, finish typing Kucharsky's name and the colon. Press [Enter] twice again. So far, your letter should look like Figure 3-28.

6. Click Tools, then click AutoCorrect Options to open the AutoCorrect dialog box with the AutoCorrect tab displayed. In the Replace box, type the letters sm (lowercase letters). In the With box, type SMCSL-NRD (uppercase letters). Click [Add] to add the entry to the scrollable list of AutoCorrect entries. To accept the new entry and close the dialog box, click [OK]. Whenever you type the letters sm and a space, Word automatically will convert the letters to SMCSL-NRD. See Figure 3-24 for a screen shot of the AutoCorrect dialog box.

(continued on WD 3.28)

Figure 3-28 Date, inside address, and salutation of letter

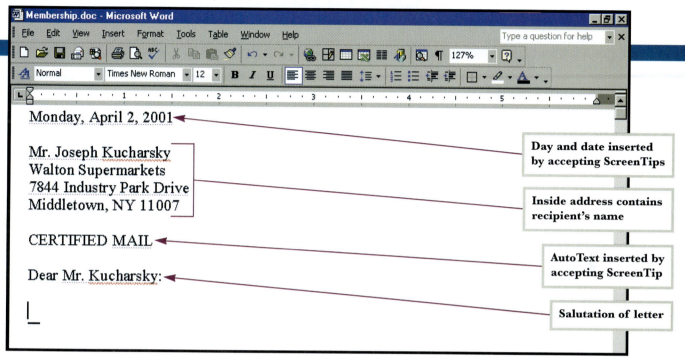

Figure 3-29 Body of letter, membership.doc

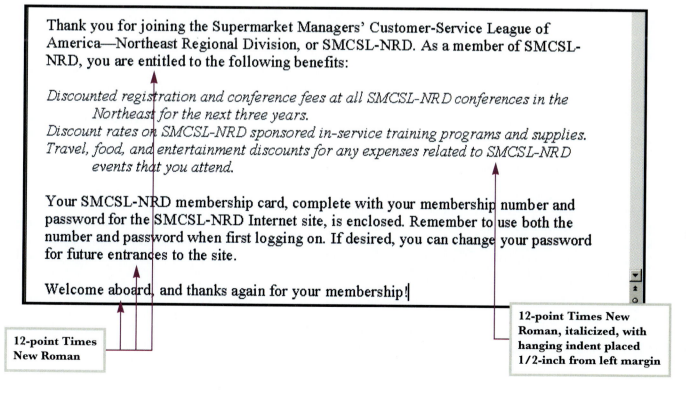

skill: Inserting Frequently Used Text (continued)

do it!

7. Type and format the body of the letter as shown in Figure 3-29 (on the previous page). However, instead of typing the capital letters SMCSL-NRD, be sure to type the two lowercase letters sm and a space. Word automatically will change the lowercase letters to the eight capitalized ones. When finished typing all of the text in Figure 3-29, press [Enter] twice.

8. Click the View menu, click the Toolbars command and click AutoText to turn on the Autotext toolbar. Click the All Entries arrow, click the Closing category, and click Sincerely yours, to insert the two words and a comma as a closing (see Figure 3-30). Press [Enter] four times.

9. Type your first and last names as a signature line, and press [Enter]. Type the following text to complete the closing address, remembering to type just the lowercase letters sm and a space in place of the eight capitalized letters:

    SMCSL-NRD Director
    687 Marlboro Blvd.
    Marlboro, MA 02345

10. The closing of your document should look like Figure 3-31. Proofread, re-save, and close the document, Membership.doc.

more

In the Skill above you used the AutoText tab of the AutoCorrect dialog box to insert two pre-existing AutoText entries that might appear often in standard documents such as memos, letters, and the like. Some AutoText entries automatically include data that relates to the document. For example, if the insertion point is on the fourth page of a ten-page document and you insert the AutoText entry Page X of Y, Word will insert Page 4 of 10. You also used the AutoCorrect tab to create a new entry for frequently used text, using the shortened version of the entry to enter its longer version in a document. Just as you used the AutoCorrect tab to create a new entry, so also can you use the AutoText tab to do so (see Figure 3-32). To create an entry, you would type it in the box labeled Enter AutoText entries here. Once you created the entry, it would appear alphabetized in the scrollable box immediately below the labeled box. Additionally, when you clicked on the entry in the scrollable box, the first few lines (if any) of the entry would appear in the Preview box immediately below the scrollable box.

You also can create a new AutoText entry so that it includes graphics as well as text. To do so, begin by typing the entry in a document. Then highlight precisely that part of the entry, including any graphics you created, that you want to store as AutoText. (If you created a paragraph and wanted to include its formatting, be sure to highlight the paragraph mark too.) Next, click Insert, click AutoText, and then click New to open the Create AutoText dialog box. In this dialog box either accept the entry name that appears in the box labeled Please name your AutoText entry or type a new name. To accept the new entry and close the dialog box, press [Enter] or click OK.

Once you close the dialog box, you can access the new entry through either the AutoText toolbar or the AutoText tab in the AutoCorrect dialog box. The name of the new entry appearing on the toolbar or in the dialog box will match the name you gave it in the Create AutoText dialog box. As suggested above, the Preview box of the AutoText tab will display how the AutoText will look in a document, including formatting features such as font style, line spacing, underlining, and so on. However, you can preview only the first few lines, or about 30 to 40 words, of text.

Figure 3-30 AutoText toolbar, "Sincerely yours," option selected

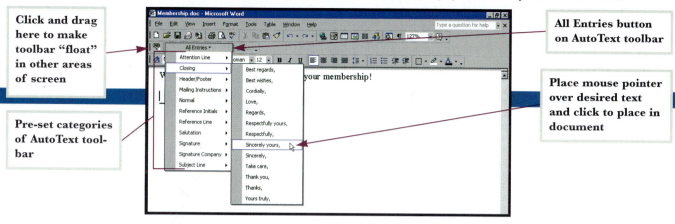

- Click and drag here to make toolbar "float" in other areas of screen
- Pre-set categories of AutoText toolbar
- All Entries button on AutoText toolbar
- Place mouse pointer over desired text and click to place in document

Figure 3-31 Closing of letter, Membership.doc

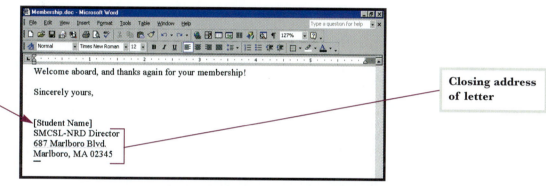

- Type your name on signature line (without brackets)
- Closing address of letter

Figure 3-32 AutoText tab of AutoCorrect dialog box

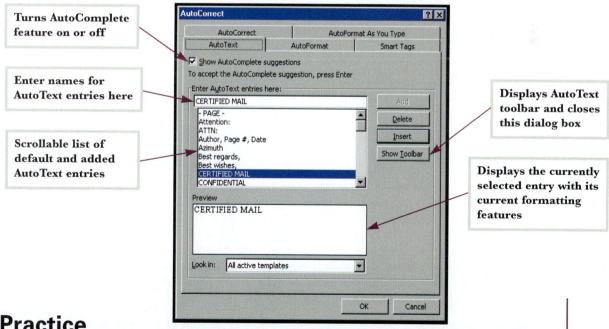

- Turns AutoComplete feature on or off
- Enter names for AutoText entries here
- Scrollable list of default and added AutoText entries
- Displays AutoText toolbar and closes this dialog box
- Displays the currently selected entry with its current formatting features

Practice

Open Student File wdprac3-11.doc and save it in your Word Files folder as mywdprac3-11.doc. Following the instructions that appear at the beginning of the file, practice inserting frequently used text based on an entry that you have created in the AutoCorrect dialog box. When you finish typing the paragraph in the file, save it again as mywdprac3-11.doc, and then delete the new entry you created in the dialog box.

skill — Using the Word Thesaurus

concept

Word has a Thesaurus feature, which is a reference tool that supplies you with synonyms (words with similar meanings) and antonyms (words with opposite meanings) for a word that you select in a document. In the Thesaurus dialog box, Word highlights a word that most closely matches the meaning of the word you selected. You then can replace the selected word with the other word, search for even a more precise word to match your desired meaning, or explore the meanings of the antonyms.

do it!

Use the Thesaurus feature to choose a more precise word for a word selected in a document.

1. Open the Student File wddoit3-12.doc and save it in your Word Files folder as Report12.doc.

2. Select or just click on the word hard in the third paragraph, fifth sentence, of the report—the sentence that begins Many telecommuters are not....

3. Click Tools, click Language, and then click Thesaurus to open the Thesaurus dialog box (or press the keyboard shortcut [Shift]+[F7]). The word that you selected will display in the Looked Up box in the upper left area of the dialog box (see Figure 3-33).

4. In the scrollable box immediately below the Replace with Synonym box, click the word inflexible.

5. Click [Look Up] to search for synonyms of inflexible, and click the word rigid that displays in the scrollable list box immediately below the Replace with Synonym box.

6. Click [Replace] to insert the word rigid in place of hard in the report. Save and close your document, Report12.doc, with your change.

more

When the Thesaurus dialog box opens, the Looked up box displays the word or phrase you just selected in a document. If you open the dialog box but have not selected a word, the Looked up box displays the word you most recently looked up. (If your selected word does not match any word in the Thesaurus, the Looked up box changes to a Not found box.) The Meanings box displays synonyms matching the word in the Looked up box. (If Word cannot find any words that seem like proper synonyms, the Meanings box will display, in alphabetic order, just a list of words spelled similarly to the selected word.) The Replace with Synonym box displays either the selected word from the Meanings box or from the scrollable list box immediately below the Replace with Synonym box, whichever you clicked last. The scrollable list box supplies synonyms (and a few antonyms) for the word selected in the Meanings box, just as the Meanings box displays synonyms for the word in the Looked up box. For quick access to synonyms for a word, right-click the word. The shortcut menu that appears will include a Synonyms command that offers suggested synonyms for the word you right-clicked and access to the Thesaraus dialog box.

As you choose the best words to put in your document, or after you have finished all your typing, you may want to know how many words you have typed overall. To do so, you can use the Word Count dialog box (see Figure 3-34) or the Word Count toolbar. (This toolbar, shown in Figure 3-35, is a new feature in Word 2002.). To open the Word Count dialog box, click Tools, and then click Word Count. The Word Count dialog box also displays the number of pages, characters, paragraphs, and lines in your document. To display the Word Count toolbar, you can click [Show Toolbar] in the lower left corner of the Word Count dialog box. Otherwise, you can click View, click Toolbars, and then click Word Count and view the same statistics there. The advantage of the toolbar is that you periodically can click [Recount] as you type to update yourself on the statistics of the active document.

Figure 3-33 Thesaurus dialog box

- Displays word or phrase selected in document
- Highlight word that best matches meaning of word in Looked Up box; more synonyms will appear in scrollable box to right
- Replaces Looked Up word with word highlighted in scrollable box
- This word will replace word in Looked Up box
- Scroll through choices and click one to place it in Replace with Synonym box
- Retrieves list of synonyms for highlighted word in scrollable box

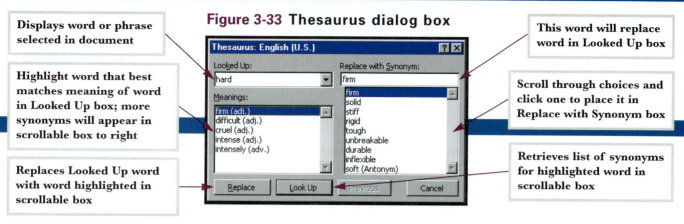

Figure 3-34 Report12.doc, after replacing text

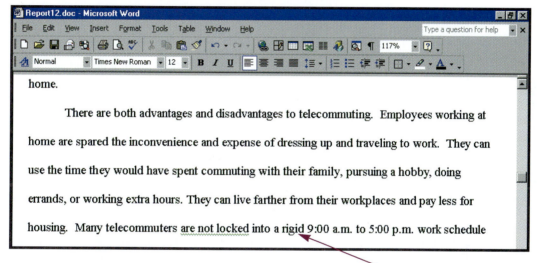

- Word from Replace with Synonym box replaces originally selected word

Figure 3-35 Word Count dialog box

- Statistics for the active document
- Adds footnote and endnote statistics to totals
- Displays Word Count toolbar

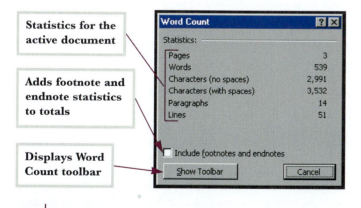

Figure 3-36 Word Count toolbar

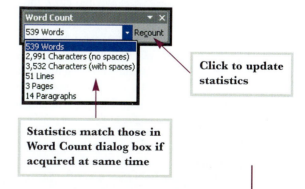

- Click to update statistics
- Statistics match those in Word Count dialog box if acquired at same time

Practice

Open Student File **wdprac3-12.doc** and save it in your Word Files folder as **mywdprac3-12.doc**. Following the instructions at the beginning of the file, practice using the Thesaurus dialog box to find more precise words for the ones that are identified in the practice file. When you have completed the practice exercise, resave and close **mywdprac3-12.doc**.

skill: Finding and Replacing Text

concept

The Find command enables you to search a document for individual occurrences of any word, phrase, or other unit of text. The Replace command enables you to replace one or all occurrences of a word that you have found. Together, the Find and Replace commands form powerful editing tools for making many extensive changes in just seconds.

do it!

Use Find and Replace to spell a word consistently throughout a document.

1. Open Student File wddoit3-13.doc and save it in your Word Files folder as Report13.doc.

2. If necessary, place the insertion point at the beginning of the document. Word will search the document from the insertion point forward.

3. Click Edit, and then click Replace. The Find and Replace dialog box appears with the Replace tab in front and the insertion point in the Find What text box.

4. In the Find What box, type the two words per cent. Click in the Replace With box, and type the one word percent (see Figure 3-37).

5. Click [Replace All] to search the document for all instances of per cent and to replace them with percent. A message box appears to display the results. In this case, one replacement was made (see Figure 3-38). In short documents the Find and Replace procedure takes so little time that you usually cannot cancel it before it ends. However, in longer documents you can cancel a search in progress by pressing [Esc].

6. Click [OK] to close the message box. Click [Close] to close the Find and Replace dialog box.

7. Save and close the document, Report13.doc, with your change.

more

Clicking the Replace All button in the Find and Replace dialog box replaces every instance of the text you have placed in the Find What box. To examine and replace a word or phrase manually instead of automatically, start by clicking the Find Next button. If you desire to replace that instance, click the Replace button. Continue checking the document like this, clicking the Find Next button and then, if desired, the Replace button. Keep clicking the pairs of buttons until you have run through the entire document. Unless you absolutely must do otherwise, use this method for shorter documents only.

The first button under the Replace With box usually displays the word More. Click this button when you want to display the Search Options area of the dialog box. With the area displayed, the More button converts to a Less button. Clicking on the Less button will hide the Search Options area. The Search drop-down list under Search Options determines the direction of the search relative to the insertion point. You can search upward or downward through the document or keep the Word default setting of All to check the whole document, including headers, footers, and footnotes. The Format drop-down list enables you to include search criteria for fonts, paragraphs, tabs, and similar items. The Special drop-down list enables you to search for paragraph marks, tab characters, column breaks and related special characters. The No Formatting button removes all formatting criteria from searches. For information on the Search Option activated by the check boxes, consult Table 3-3.

The Find tab of the Find and Replace dialog box matches the Replace tab except it lacks the replace function and only searches documents for items that you specify.

Figure 3-37 Find and Replace dialog box

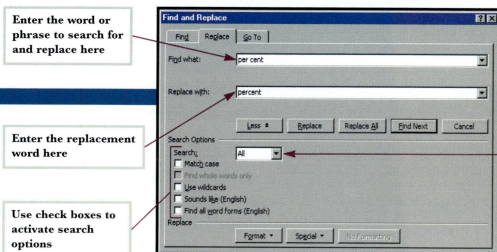

- Enter the word or phrase to search for and replace here
- Enter the replacement word here
- Use check boxes to activate search options
- Click to determine direction of search

Figure 3-38 Report13.doc, after Find and Replace activity

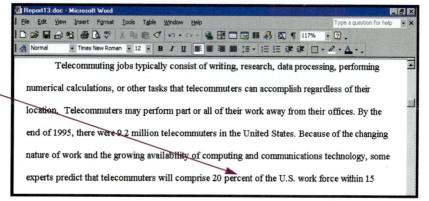

- Find and Replace makes one change in document

Table 3-3 Search Options

Option	Description
Match case	Finds those items in capitals and/or lowercase that exactly match contents of Find What box
Find whole words only	Finds only those items that are whole words, not parts of a larger word
Use wildcards	Searches for wildcards, special characters, or special search operators found in Find What box
Sounds like	Finds words that sound the same as in Find What box but are spelled differently
Find all word forms	Replaces all forms of the text in Find What box with proper forms of the word in the Replace with box; words in both boxes should be the same part of speech

Practice

Open Student File wdprac3-13.doc and save it in your Word Files folder as mywdprac3-13.doc. Following the instructions that appear at the beginning of the file, practice using the Find and Replace dialog box to search for and replace text. When you have completed the practice exercise, resave and close mywdprac3-13.doc.

shortcuts

Function	Button/Mouse	Menu	Keyboard	
Adjust margins		Click File, then click Page Setup		
Indent selected paragraph[s]	Click and drag indent markers on the Horizontal toolbar	Click Format, then click Paragraph, then click the Indents and Spacing tab, then click Special box	[Ctrl]+[M] [Ctrl]+[T]	(Entire) (Hanging)
Adjust Line Spacing of selected paragraph[s]		Click Format, then click Paragraph, then click the Indents and Spacing tab, then click Line spacing box	[Ctrl]+[1] [Ctrl]+[2] [Ctrl]+[5]	(Single) (Double) (1.5)
Go to the next window (when working with multiple documents)	Click on the part of the next window that is showing, if the active window is not maximized	Click Window, then click the name of the next document	[Ctrl]+[F6]	
Go to the previous window (when working with multiple documents)	Click on the part of the previous window that is showing, if the active window is not maximized	Click Window, then click the name of the previous document	[Ctrl]+[Shift]+[F6]	
Use Format Painter	(icon)		[Ctrl]+[Shift]+[C]	
Check for spelling and grammar errors	(icon)	Click Tools, then click Spelling and Grammar	[F7]	
Find next misspelling (with Automatic Spell Checking active)	Scroll down in the document to the next word with a wavy red underline		[Alt]+[F7]	
Find next grammatical error (with Automatic Grammar Checking active)	Scroll down in the document to the next word with a wavy green underline		[Alt]+[F7]	
Insert new AutoText		Click Insert, then click AutoText, then click New	[Alt]+[F3]	
Open the Word Thesaurus	Right-click a word, then point to Synonyms on the pop-up menu	Click Tools, then click Language, then click Thesaurus	[Shift]+[F7]	

A. Identify Key Features

Name the items indicated by callouts in Figure 3-39.

Figure 3-39 Identifying formatting and editing concepts

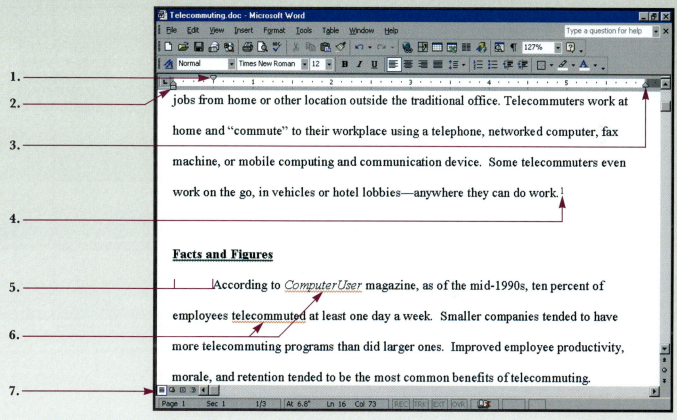

1.
2.
3.
4.
5.
6.
7.

B. Select the Best Answer

8. Objects that slide along the horizontal ruler and determine text placement
9. A Word feature that fixes common typographic mistakes as they are made
10. Markers that recognize and label data that the markers can manipulate
11. Displays the number of words, characters, paragraphs, etc. in your document
12. The invisible line marking the boundary between text and the edge of a page
13. A feature that finds synonyms and antonyms for a selected word or phrase
14. The window where footnotes and endnotes appear while in Normal view

a. Thesaurus
b. Indent markers
c. Notes pane
d. Margin
e. Word Count dialog box
f. Smart Tags
g. AutoCorrect

quiz (continued)

C. Complete the Statement

15. Document-level formatting includes:
    a. Indents
    b. Fonts
    c. Margins
    d. Footnotes

16. When a page has no more room for text and you then enter more text, Word automatically creates a:
    a. New document based on the Normal template
    b. Manual page break
    c. Drop-down list
    d. Soft page break

17. A note reference mark is:
    a. A mark in the text referring to a footnote or endnote
    b. Another name for a tab stop
    c. Text that has been highlighted
    d. An encyclopedia on floppy disk or CD-ROM

18. AutoCorrect fixes spelling mistakes when you press [Enter], enter a punctuation mark, or
    a. Press the space bar
    b. Save the document
    c. Turn on Automatic Spell Checking
    d. Access the Spelling/Thesaurus toolbar

19. Paragraph-level formatting includes:
    a. Page numbers
    b. Headers and footers
    c. Italics
    d. Line spacing

20. To view page numbers, switch to:
    a. Normal view
    b. Print Layout view
    c. Full Screen view
    d. Mirror margins

21. One way to copy text from one document to another is to:
    a. Set up File Sharing on the Control Panel
    b. Click while pressing [F11]
    c. Use the Clipboard
    d. Use the Style Gallery

22. The ✏️ button:
    a. Adds color to all black text
    b. Copies formatting from one area to another
    c. Pastes Clipboard contents into a document
    d. Displays or hides the Drawing toolbar

23. To leave the first line of a paragraph against the left margin while indenting all of its other lines, apply a:
    a. Dangling indent
    b. First-line indent
    c. Tabbing indent
    d. Hanging indent

24. The AutoCorrect dialog box does **not** contain:
    a. The AutoCorrect tab
    b. The AutoRepair tab
    c. The AutoFormat tab
    d. The Smart Tags tab

Build Your Skills

1. Open a document and format it.

   a. Open the student file, wdskills3.doc, and save it to your student disk as Huntly1.doc.

   b. Open the Page Setup dialog box on the File menu.

   c. Set the left and right margins at 1 inch. Insert page numbers at the bottom center of the page.

2. Apply indents to the document, change the line spacing, and insert a footnote:

   a. Select all of the text in the document below the title.

   b. From the Paragraph dialog box on the Format menu, apply a first line indent of .5 inches and change the line spacing to double.

   c. Insert a footnote after (43) in paragraph 2, line 5 of the document. The footnote should read All quotes refer to the revised 1862 edition of the book.

3. Adjust the alignment and text formatting of the document:

   a. Select all of the text in the document below the title and justify it. Select the title and center it.

   b. Add bold formatting to the student author's name and to the title of the paper.

   c. Re-save the document, but do not close it.

4. Open another document and copy text from it into the original document:

   a. Open the student file wdskills3a.doc and select the paragraph it contains. It is the conclusion to the paper used above.

   b. Copy the selected paragraph to the Clipboard.

   c. Close student file, wdskills3a.doc, bringing back Huntly1.doc as the active window.

   d. Place the insertion point at the very end of the document.

   e. Paste the copied paragraph onto the end of the paper, being sure it begins on a new line as a new paragraph.

5. Use the Format Painter to change the formatting of the inserted paragraph to match the rest of the document:

   a. Select the next-to-last paragraph in the document by triple-clicking it.

   b. Click the Format Painter button to copy the formatting of the selected paragraph.

   c. Drag the I-beam (which now has a paintbrush icon next to it) across the last paragraph in the document to select it and match its formatting with that of the previous paragraph.

   d. Click once in the paragraph to deselect it.

interactivity (continued)

Build Your Skills

6. Check for spelling errors and replace all instances of one word with another.

    a. Click the Tools menu, then click Spelling and Grammar to open the Spelling and Grammar dialog box. Clear the Check grammar check box so you will check for only spelling errors.

    b. Correct the three misspelled words in the document, ignoring names and unusual words.

    c. Click Edit, then click Replace to open the Find and Replace dialog box.

    d. Use the Replace all command to replace all instances of Browne with the correct name, Brown.

    e. Close the dialog box, and save the document as Huntly2.doc, and close it.

7. Add a spelling correction and an entry for frequently used text using the AutoCorrect tab of the AutoCorrect dialog box.

    a. Open a new, blank document, and open the AutoCorrect dialog box.

    b. Use the Replace and With boxes on the AutoCorrect tab to instruct Word to replace instances of clcik with click. On the same tab, instruct Word to replace the shortened text rd with the longer entry Rough Draft.

    d. Close the dialog box, and type the following sentence exactly as it appears: Use a mouse clcik to open rd files, and use the same mouse clcik to close the rd files. Verify that your two new AutoCorrect entries converted to correctly spelled text.

    e. Return to the AutoCorrect tab, delete the two entries you created, and close the dialog box.

    f. Save the one-sentence file to your student disk as autocorrect.doc. Close the file.

Problem Solving Exercises

1. Using the skills you learned in Lesson 3, open the student file, wdproblem3-1.doc, and save it as custom.doc. Change the left and right margins to 1.25 inches. For all text below the title, apply a first-line indent of .5 inches, and change the line spacing to 1.5. Add page numbers to the top, center area of the pages, starting on page 1. Center and boldface the title, and justify the main body text of the document. Insert three footnotes into the paper. (The text of the footnotes appears in the student file wdproblem3-1a.doc.) Insert the first footnote at the end of the third paragraph, following the period after the word products. Insert the second footnote at the end of the fourth paragraph, following the period after the word inventory. Insert the third footnote at the end of the sixth paragraph, after the period after the word line. Open Spell Checking and correct all misspellings in the document. Add your name, your instructor's name, and the due date at the top, left side of page 1, observing the same revised line spacing as in the body of the document. Re-save the document, custom.doc, and close the file.

2. You are applying for a position as either a movie reviewer or restaurant critic, and you want to practice your reviewing skills before your interview. Review either your three favorite movies or three favorite fast-food restaurants in a three-paragraph, one-page document, and save the document as reviews.doc. Set up the document with 1 inch margins on all sides. After you enter all of your text, insert a Continuous Section break between the first and second, and between the second and third paragraphs. Format the first paragraph with 12-point, italicized Times New Roman text and a .5-inch, hanging indent. Format the second paragraph with 11-point Arial text and a .5-inch, first-line indent. Format the third paragraph exactly as the first. At the top, left side of page 1, add your name, instructor's name, and due date. Also add a centered title. Double-space after the due date and after the title, but keep all other line spacing at single spacing. Re-save the document, reviews.doc, and close the file.

interactivity (continued)

Problem Solving Exercises (continued)

3. Open the file wdproblem3-3.doc and save it as Westerner.doc. On the first line of the document, replace the words [Student Name] with your own name. Replace the default date of the document with the due date of this assignment. Eliminate the double-spacing between paragraphs and indent each paragraph instead with a first-line indent. Change the whole document to double-spacing. Add a page number to the bottom center of only page 2. Find and replace all instances of Lindberg with Lindbergh. Correct the spelling of the four remaining misspelled words. Save the changes you have made to the document, print it, and close the file.

4. Open the file wdproblem3-4.doc and save it as Handout.doc. Reformat the document so it resembles the one that appears below in Figure 3-40. This reformatting will involve changing the margins, centering some text, justifying other text, changing the font sizes of the sections, and adding a footnote. The footnote should say For information, contact Beatrice Jones, Head Librarian of the Slattery Public Library at 515-555-5445 during normal library hours. In the footnote, replace the Head Librarian's name with your own first and last names. After reformatting the document, use Find and Replace to change all occurrences of Slatery to Slattery and all occurrences of Libary to Library. Save the changes you have made to the document, verify that it looks like the document below, and then print and close and the file.

Figure 3-40 Identifying formatting and editing concepts

> Monday, January 1, 2002
> Tuesday, January 2, 2002
>
> Slattery Public Library
> 125 Division Street, Slattery, TX
>
> Come one, come all to the
> **FIFTH ANNUAL**
> **Slattery Public Library Book Sale**
>
> The Library sale will include over 10,000 (count 'em, 10,000) used hardback and paperback books, starting as low as 50 cents for paperbacks and one dollar for hardbacks. A specialized mix of antiquarian, rare, and first-edition books will be sold under a written bid system, with ties on pricing going to the earliest bidder. The Library's rare book consultant will be on site on Friday evening only to verify the authenticity and condition of these special books.
>
> All proceeds from the sale will go to the Library's Redding Fund for Literacy Training and the Slattery Memorial Development Fund for the new children's wing, to start construction early next year. Persons wishing to make tax-deductible donations to either fund may do so at any time during the book sale. Cash and check will be accepted. (Persons donating cash will receive a written receipt from the Library treasurer on the spot.)
>
> *Persons wishing to make book donations for this sale also will receive a tax deduction for a portion of the purchase price of the book, depending on condition and estimated popularity of the item.*[1]
>
> ---
> [1] For more information, contact Beatrice Jones, Head Librarian of the Slattery Public Library at 515-555-5445 during normal business hours.

Tables and Charts

To present information in a document in an organized and easily understood fashion, you often can structure your data in the form of a table or chart. Word makes it easy to create, modify, and format tables in its documents. Word enables you to perform many of the more complex tasks associated with tables, such as calculating and sorting, that computer users often find only in dedicated worksheet programs.

Word can create blank tables into which you enter data, or you can transform existing data directly into table form. Once you have created a table, you quickly can insert or delete data as needed or reorganize it to communicate your point more efficiently and effectively.

Sometimes, your tables may contain so much data or textual information that readers may have trouble gleaning important facts or trends from them. In these cases you would do well to present the data in graphic form via a chart so readers will be able to grasp more readily the significance of your data. Fortunately, just as Word has the features you need to create helpful tables, the program has the features it takes to create, modify, and format charts with relative ease and efficiency.

Lesson Goal:

You will open a file that will benefit from the presence of a table, create and modify that table, and learn various ways to format the table. You will learn how to create a chart based on a table, modify and format it, and insert it in a report. You also will learn an alternate way to create tables and format them for ease of reading and attractiveness.

- Inserting and Modifying a Table
- Editing Tables
- Inserting and Deleting Rows, Columns, and Cells
- Sorting Data in a Table
- Calculating Data in a Table
- Formatting a Table
- Creating a Chart
- Editing a Chart
- Drawing a Table
- Adding Borders and Shading

skill: Creating and Modifying Tables

concept

A table consists of information organized into horizontal rows and vertical columns. The box created by an intersecting row and column is a cell. You can create a table from scratch or assemble it from existing text. Tables often have row and column headers, which are labels to identify the adjacent data. Data in a table can consist of words (also called labels) or numbers (also called values).

do it!

Insert a table into a pre-existing report to organize information difficult to describe in words.

1. Open Student File wddoit4-1.doc and save it in your Word Files folder as Matthews.doc.

2. Scroll down to the third paragraph, which begins Regarding handicapped people with…. Place the insertion point at the end of the paragraph, after the colon that comes after the word disabilities.

3. Click the Insert Table button on the Standard toolbar. A table grid appears, enabling you to select the number of rows and columns that will appear in your table.

4. Gradually move the mouse pointer from the upper left toward the lower right of the grid until you have selected an area of boxes that is two rows deep and four columns wide. The text 2 x 4 Table appears in the rectangular area below the grid to confirm that you have selected the properly sized table (see Figure 4-1).

5. Click the mouse button to insert a table into the report. The table appears on the next line of the document. Black gridlines delineate where the rows and columns are located, end-of-cell marks delineate the end of text in each cell, and end-of-row marks delineate where the last column in a row resides (see Figure 4-2). If the cell marks do not appear, turn on the Show/Hide button on the Standard toolbar.

6. The final table for the report will be single-spaced and have four rows and five columns, but you now have only two double-spaced rows and four columns. The rows are double-spaced because the text into which the table was inserted uses this spacing. Click Table on the Menu bar, highlight the Select command, and then click Table on the Select sub-menu to select the entire table. Press [Ctrl]+[1] to change the table from double to single spacing.

7. With the entire table still selected, click Table, and then click Split Cells to display the Split Cells dialog box. Since the Number of columns box already is highlighted, just type 5. Press [Tab] to move to the Number of rows box, and press 4 (see Figure 4-3). Be sure that a check mark appears in Merge cells before split check box. Click OK to close the dialog box and to reformat the table at four rows high by five columns across.

8. The final version of Row 1 will need only three columns, so you must merge some cells. Select the second and third cells in the first row. Click Table, then click Merge Cells. Select the last two cells in the first row, click Table, then click Merge Cells. Row 1 now has three columns, while the remaining three rows have five. Do not worry about the irregular column widths, as you will reformat the columns shortly.

(continued on WD 4.4)

Figure 4-1 Using the Insert Table button

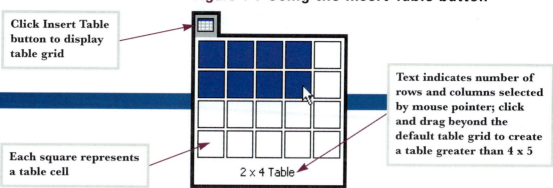

Click Insert Table button to display table grid

Text indicates number of rows and columns selected by mouse pointer; click and drag beyond the default table grid to create a table greater than 4 x 5

Each square represents a table cell

Figure 4-2 Table inserted in Word document, matthews.doc

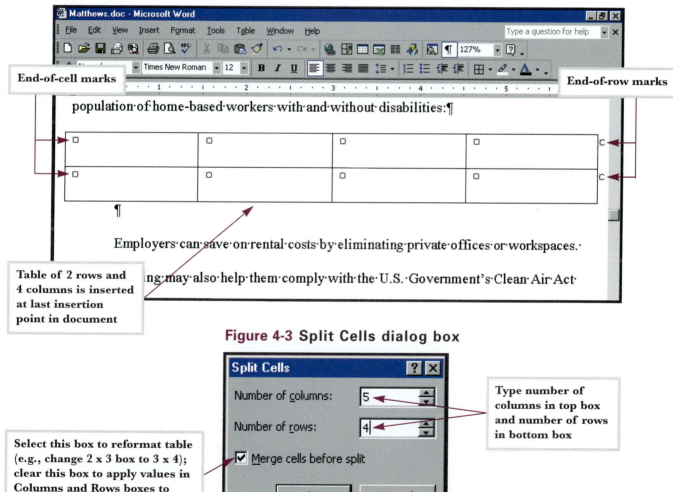

End-of-cell marks

End-of-row marks

Table of 2 rows and 4 columns is inserted at last insertion point in document

Figure 4-3 Split Cells dialog box

Type number of columns in top box and number of rows in bottom box

Select this box to reformat table (e.g., change 2 x 3 box to 3 x 4); clear this box to apply values in Columns and Rows boxes to selected cells individually

skill Creating and Modifying Tables (continued)

do it !

9. Since the table now has the required columns in each row, you can start entering text. Click in Row 1, Column 1, and type Percent Doing Any Paid Telecommuting If In. Click in Row 1, Column 2 (the first area of merged cells), and type Disabilities. Click in Row 1, Column 3 (the second area of merged cells), and type No Disabilities. Again, do not worry about formatting.

10. With your insertion point at the end of the text in the last column of Row 1, look at Figure 4-4. Fill in the rest of the table with the text that appears in the figure. Begin by pressing [Tab] to move to Row 2, Column 1. Type the words Private Sector, and press [Tab] to move to Row 2, Column 2. Repeat this typing and tabbing process until you enter all needed text in the table. Once again, do not worry about formatting.

11. Next, arrange the table so it looks attractive and does not use up excess white space. Begin by clicking anywhere in the table. Click Table, click AutoFit, and then click AutoFit to Contents. Also click Table, click Select, click Table, and click the Center button. The first column has widened to place its text on one line, the rest of the columns have narrowed to eliminate unneeded white space, and the overall table is centered on the page.

12. Percentages, dollar amounts, and a lot of other numerical data often contain decimal points, which generally should be vertically aligned. Select the 12 lower right cells in the table, starting with Row 2, Column 2 (with the text 2.1%) and ending with the lower right cell of the table (with the text 52.6%).

13. Click the Align Right button. Since only one decimal place and the percent symbol appear to the right of all the decimals, all of them align vertically. Click the Show/Hide button to turn it off, and click outside the table (see Figure 4-5). You also can align decimals as follows: highlight the cells that need aligning, click the tab alignment marker at the left end of the Horizontal Ruler until it changes to a decimal tab, and then click on the ruler above the related column where you want the decimals to align.

14. Save and close your document with the changes you have made.

more

Besides creating tables with the Insert Table button, you can click Table, click Insert, and click Table to open the Insert Table dialog box. Like the Insert Table button, the dialog box enables you to select the number of columns and rows for new tables. However, this dialog box also enables you to set specific column widths, autofit tables to their contents or within Web browser windows, access the Table AutoFormat dialog box (explained later in this lesson), and so on. If you have pre-existing text in a document, you can convert it to a table by highlighting the text and clicking the Insert Table button. Table cells are determined by tabs and paragraphs in the highlighted text. Another way to create a table from text is to highlight the text, click Table, click Convert, and click Text to Table to open the Convert Text to Table dialog box, which resembles the Insert Table dialog box. Whichever way you create tables, you can modify their text and formatting through the Tables and Borders toolbar (see Figure 4-6).

As part of Microsoft Office, Word enables you to insert tables from other programs. For example, you can create linked objects and embedded objects. Linked objects are created in source files from programs like Excel or Access and then inserted into destination files like Word. Linked objects maintain a connection, or link, between the source and destination files. Because of this link objects in destination files will update whenever you update them in source files. Embedded objects resemble linked objects because both are created in source files and then inserted into destination files. However, once inserted in a destination file, the embedded object becomes part of that file. Changes made to the embedded object are, therefore, part of the destination file only and not part of the source file. Such sharing of files increases the power and flexibility of all of the Office programs.

Figure 4-4 Table with text, before formatting

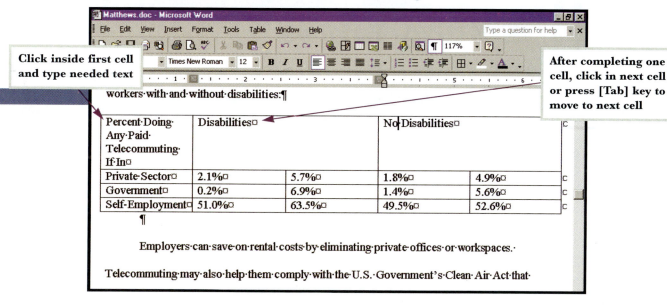

Figure 4-5 Table with text, after formatting

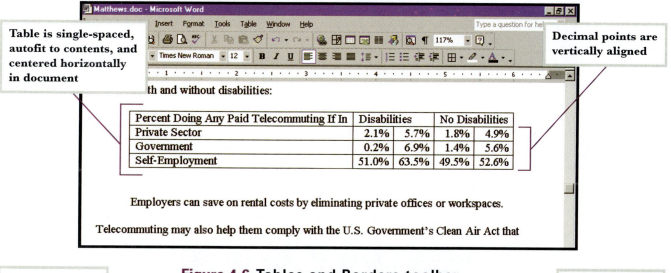

Figure 4-6 Tables and Borders toolbar

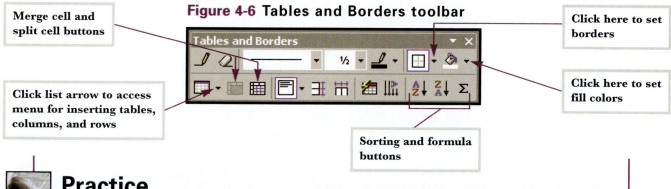

Practice

To practice creating tables, open Student File wdprac4-1.doc. Save and close any changes you make in your Word Files folder as mywdprac4-1.doc.

skill Editing Tables

concept

Once you have entered text and modified the format of a table, often the table still does not have all the text or formatting features that you need or want. Therefore, Word makes it as easy to edit text in cells as in regular areas of a document. Likewise, the program also offers many features for modifying formatting even further. The next few Skills focus on these text editing and table formatting features.

do it!

Change headings in a table and modify their format.

1. Open Student File wddoit4-2.doc and save it in your Word Files folder as lee.doc. Scroll down to the table that appears between the second and third paragraphs.

2. Position the insertion point just after the word Total in the table. Type a space, then type (in Millions) to complete the heading.

3. Press [Tab] to move to the next cell to the right. All the information in the cell is selected. Click immediately to the left of the word at to deselect the cell and to position the insertion point there. Type Working and press [Spacebar] to complete the cell heading.

4. Select all the headings in the table. Click the Center button to align the text horizontally in the header cells. Alternately, you can align text by using the Table and Borders toolbar. Display the toolbar by clicking View, clicking Toolbars, and then clicking Tables and Borders. (Or right-click in a gray area of the toolbars and click Tables and Borders.) After the toolbar displays, click the Align button arrow to display the Cell Alignment palette. Without clicking the mouse button, move the mouse pointer over the nine buttons to see where each one would place text. When finished, click the Align Top Center icon to center the text horizontally at the top of the cell (see Figure 4-7).

5. Close the Tables and Buttons toolbar to get an unobstructed view of the document (see Figure 4-8). Save and close the document with your changes.

more

As the Steps above demonstrate, you can edit text in tables just as you do in regular areas of a document. You can center or align text to either side of a cell by selecting it and clicking the appropriate formatting button: Align Left, Center, or Align Right. In a table the Selection bar (the vertical area between the left edge of the screen and left margin of a page) works in much the same way as it does with text. Therefore, clicking in the Selection bar to the left of a row selects the entire row. Dragging down or up in the Selection bar adds or deletes more rows to or from the selection, depending on whether you started dragging from the top or bottom row of a table. To move a table, drag the Table Move handle, which is available at the upper-left in Print Layout View when the mouse pointer is over the table.

In tables themselves, there is a miniature Selection bar at the left edge of each cell, so clicking there will select the whole cell and not just its text. You also can select a whole cell by triple-clicking in it, whereas double-clicking in the cell will highlight just words. To select a column, place the mouse pointer over the column's top border until the mouse pointer changes to a downward arrow, then click to select the column. Dragging to the right from the leftmost column will highlight more columns, and dragging back toward the left will highlight fewer ones. To change the width of a column, place the mouse pointer over the edge of the column to display a column width pointer, click and hold the mouse button to display a vertical dotted line, and then drag the edge as needed. To automatically adjust a column to match the width of the text in that column, double-click on the right edge of the desired column. This action will adjust the column to match the width of the text, plus a bit of white space at each end of the text to make for easier reading.

Figure 4-7 Align cell text button on Tables and Borders toolbar

Click View, Toolbars, and then Tables and Borders to display toolbar

Align Cell Text button

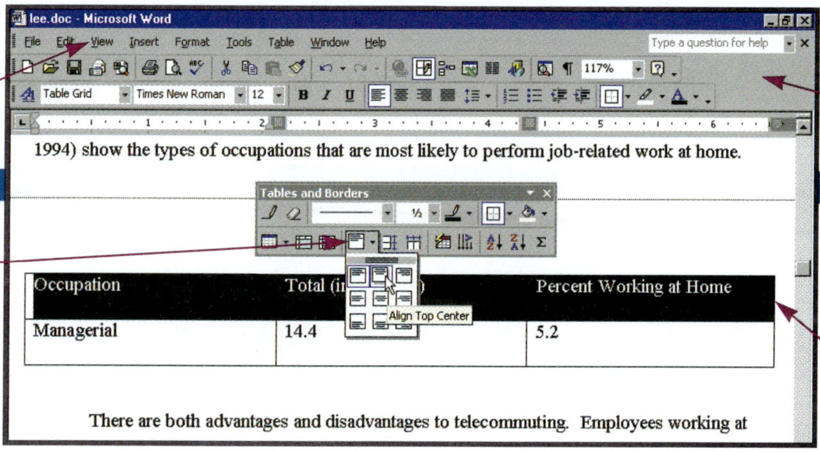

Right-click in gray area to display Toolbars menu, then click Tables and Borders

Highlight heading cells before clicking Align Cell Text button

Figure 4-8 Edited cell headings in lee.doc

Second and third cell headings are edited, and all headings are horizontally centered

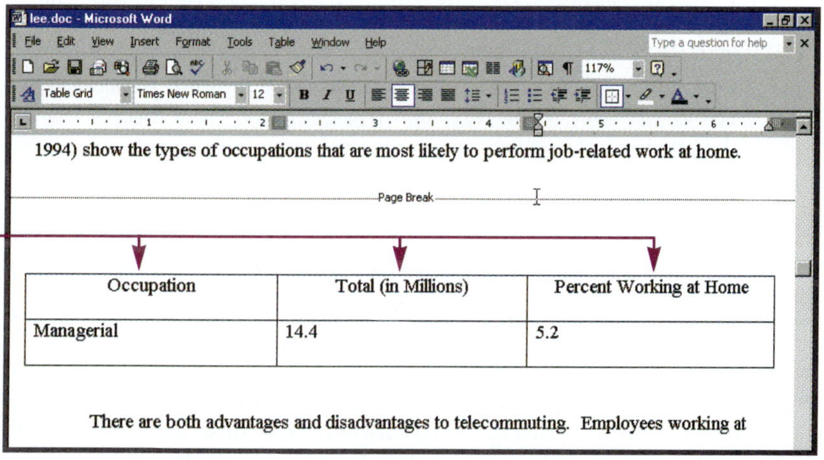

Table 4-1 Keyboard Movement and Selection Shortcuts

Desired Action	Press This
Move to next or previous cell in a table and select its contents	[Tab] or [Shift]+[Tab]
Move up or down one row	[↑] or [↓]
Move to the first or last cell in a row	[Alt]+[Home] or [Alt]+[End]
Move to the top or bottom cell in a column	[Alt]+[Pg Up] or [Alt]+[Pg Dn]
Select an entire column	[Alt]+[Click]
Select an entire table	[Alt]+[5] on the numeric keypad (with Num Lock off)

Practice

To practice editing a table, open the Student File wdprac4-2.doc. Save and close any changes you make in your Word Files folder as mywdprac4-2.doc.

Inserting and Deleting Rows, Columns, and Cells

concept

Students change their course schedules, businesses modify financial projections, people come and go in organizations, and many other changes recordable in tables occur daily in life. To handle such frequent changes to data and information, Word provides a variety of ways to facilitate adding or deleting rows, columns, and cells in tables.

do it!

Add four rows and two columns, enter data, and then delete one row and one column.

1. Open Student File wddoit4-3.doc and save it in your Word Files folder as lee-1.doc. Scroll to the table that appears between the second and third paragraphs. You eventually will expand this table to six rows and five columns. Therefore, to see the whole table during this process and improve its appearance somewhat, select the entire table now and convert it to single spacing.

2. Place the insertion point at the end of the text in the rightmost cell of the second row. Press [Tab] to create a third row below the one that just contained the insertion point.

3. Select all three rows of the table. Click Table, click Insert, and click Rows Below to add three more rows to the table, for a total of six rows.

4. Select the second and third columns of the table, either by clicking and dragging through the columns or by using the downward arrow described in the previous More section. Click Table, click Insert, and click Columns to the Right (see Figure 4-9).

5. With your insertion point in the first cell of the third row, look at Figure 4-10. Fill in the rest of the table with the text that appears in the figure.

6. At this point you decide that the data in the bottom row and the rightmost column are repetitive, so you will delete that row and column. Select all of the bottom row, click Table, click Delete, and click Rows to change the table to five rows.

7. Select all of the rightmost column, click Table, click Delete, and click Columns to change the table to four columns. Compare your table with Figure 4-11. Add or delete rows, columns, and any data as needed to conform with that figure. To delete a row or column more quickly, highlight the desired area, right-click to display a pop-up menu, and then click Delete Rows or Delete Columns. Alternately, you can select the desired area and then press [Shift]+[Delete] or [Ctrl]+[X].

8. Save and close the document with your changes.

more

Inserting or deleting cells is similar to inserting or deleting rows or columns. To insert a cell, click Table, click Insert, and then click Cells to open the Insert Cells dialog box. In this dialog box select one of four radio buttons to add a cell to the right, add a cell below the selected cell, or add an entire row or column of cells. To delete cells, click Table, click Delete, and then click Cells to open the Delete Cells dialog box. In this dialog box select one of four radio buttons to shift cells to the left, shift cells up, or delete an entire row or column of cells. Do not confuse how to delete rows, columns, and cells with how to delete text. To remove text, simply use the [Backspace] or [Delete] key to remove individual letters, or select a whole cell and press only [Delete], not [Shift]+[Delete], to remove all text in the cell.

Figure 4-9 lee-1.doc with added rows and columns

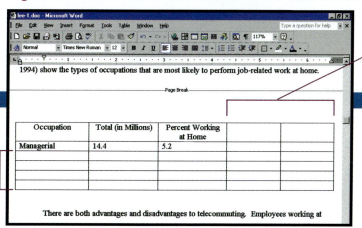

Two columns added, using the Table menu

Four rows added to table, one by tabbing and three by using Table menu

Figure 4-10 lee-1.doc with data added to new rows and columns

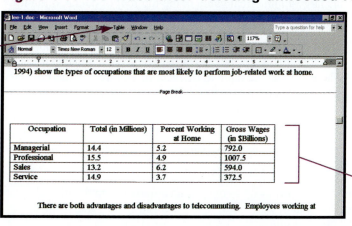

Click Table, click Insert, and then click desired command to add rows or columns

Bottom row repeats data of row above, just in slightly different form

Rightmost column repeats data in fourth column, just in slightly different form

Figure 4-11 lee-1.doc after deleting unneeded row and column

Click Table, click Delete, and click Rows or Columns to delete unneeded areas

After deleting unneeded row and column, table has 5 rows and 4 columns

Practice

To practice inserting and deleting rows and columns, open Student File wdprac4-3.doc. Save and close any changes you make in your Word Files folder as mywdprac4-3.doc.

skill: Sorting Data in a Table

concept

Word's Sort feature arranges text and data according to a pattern you can dictate. For example, when you arrange text alphabetically or arrange numbers by increasing value, you have sorted in ascending order. If you arrange text in reverse alphabetical order or arrange numbers by decreasing value, you have sorted in descending order. When you sort text and data, be sure you do so in a way that makes sense for the type of information you are sorting while making sense to your readers too. For example, you probably should sort an address list by last name then first name, but sort a mail delivery guide by street address, then house number.

do it !

List occupations in a table by their decreasing order of Working-at-Home percentage.

1. Open Student File wddoit4-4.doc and save it in your Word Files folder as lee-2.doc. Make sure the insertion point is situated somewhere in the table between the second and third paragraphs.

2. Click Table, then click Sort to open the Sort dialog box. The heading Occupation appears by default in the Sort by list box because that heading appears in the first column of the table you are working with.

3. Click the Sort by drop-down list arrow, then click Percent Working at Home. Word automatically reads all of your columns headings and includes them in the list, with the first heading as the default choice. When you chose Percent Working at Home, Word analyzed the kind of data in that column and changed the Type list box from text to number.

4. In the Sort by section, click the Descending option button so Word will sort the table with the largest numerical value in the top row of data and the lowest value in the bottom row once you close the dialog box.

5. In the My list has section, click the Header row option button if it is not already selected (see Figure 4-12). Click OK to sort the table and to close the dialog box. Click anywhere outside the table to deselect it. The data in the Percent Working at Home column now appears in descending order, the data in all other columns move to stay with their related data in the sorted column, and the heading remains at the top of the table (see Figure 4-13).

6. Save and close your document with the sorting change you have made.

more

Word allows you to sort by up to three main criteria in a table. In a table having columns for last names, first names, street addresses, cities, states, and Zip Codes, you could sort by last name, then by first name, and then by city—or you could sort by city, then by state, and then by Zip Code. Earlier versions of Word did not allow you to sort by, for example, first and last name if both types of names resided in one column. However, a new feature in Word 2002 enables you to sort by more than one word or field inside a column. If one column contained last names and first names, you could then sort by one type of name and then by the other type as well. This ability to sort by multiple fields inside a column increases the number of criteria by which you can sort.

To sort by multiple criteria, begin by clicking anywhere in your table and opening the Sort dialog box from the Table menu. Second, in the My list has section, click an option to indicate whether your table has headings across the top. Third, in the Sort by section, choose your primary sorting criterion and whether to sort in ascending or descending order. Fourth, in the upper Then by section, choose your secondary criterion, then ascending or descending order. Fifth, in the lower Then by section, choose your tertiary (or third-level) criterion, choose ascending or descending order, and then click OK.

Figure 4-12 Sort dialog box with desired sort criteria

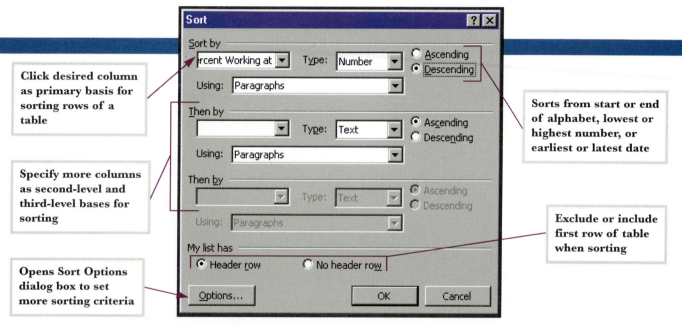

Figure 4-13 Table in lee-2.doc after sorting

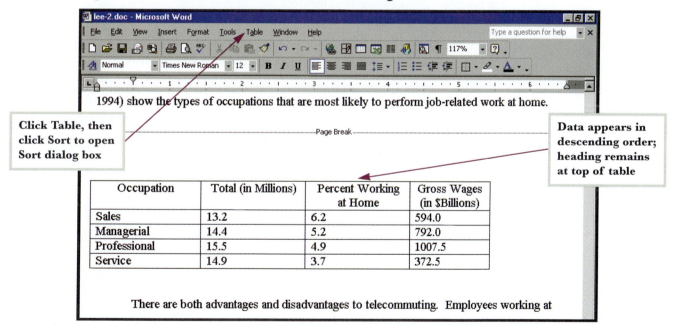

Practice

To practice sorting data in a table, open the Student File wdprac4-4.doc. Save and close any changes you make in your Word Files folder as mywdprac4-4.doc.

skill: Calculating Data in a Table

concept

The Formula command makes it easy to perform calculations in tables and comes with pre-programmed formulas such as Sum, Product, and Average. You can add formulas to the default list to meet the calculation needs of tables you create. You can design simple tables to add weekly expenses or more complex ones to calculate mortgage closing costs, thereby transforming tables from simple display objects into highly functional tools. Best of all, perhaps, mastering formulas can eliminate the worry of committing costly mathematical errors.

do it!

Automatically average the values in the Percent Working at Home column and insert the average in new cells.

1. Open Student File wddoit4-5.doc and save it in your Word Files folder as lee-3.doc.

2. Position the insertion point immediately after the number 372.5 in the rightmost cell of the bottom row of the table. Press [Tab] to create a new row.

3. In the leftmost cell of the new row, type the word Average. Press [Tab] twice. The insertion point will move two cells to the right into the empty cell at the bottom of the Percent Working at Home column (see Figure 4-14).

4. Click Table, then click Formula. The Formula dialog box will appear, with the formula =SUM(ABOVE) suggested in the Formula text box (see Figure 4-15).

5. Delete the suggested formula by selecting it and pressing [Delete]. Press [=] to place an equal sign in the empty Formula box. The equal sign at the beginning of the box tells Word that any text to follow should be treated as a formula, not as a label or value.

6. With the insertion point immediately to the right of the equal sign, click the Paste function list arrow, then click AVERAGE. The AVERAGE formula appears in the Formula text box with the insertion point between parentheses. Inside the parentheses, type C2:C5, which is the range of the cells that you want to average.

7. Look at Figure 4-16 to ensure that the formula reads =AVERAGE(C2:C5). If it does not, you can delete whatever text is in the box and simply type the formula into the Formula box, without getting the AVERAGE formula from the Paste Function box.

(continued on WD 4.14)

Figure 4-14 lee-3.doc with added row

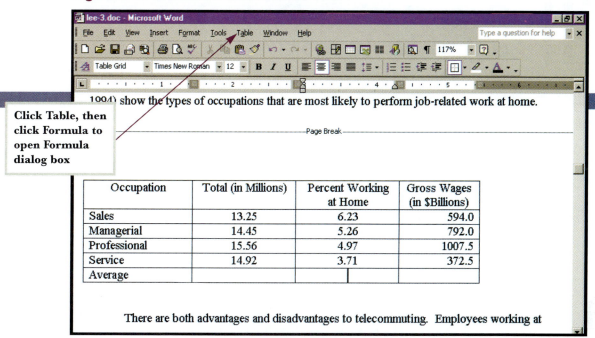

Figure 4-15 Formula dialog box with Paste Function displayed

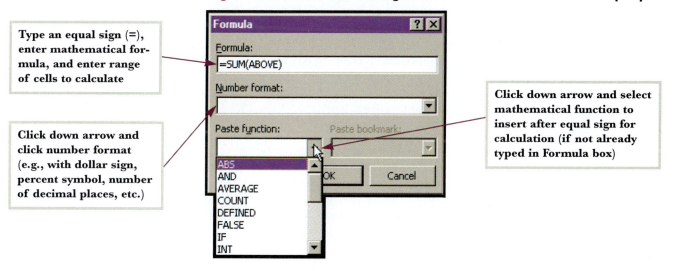

Figure 4-16 Formula dialog box with desired formula

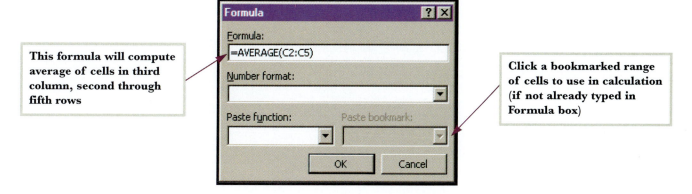

skill: Calculating Data in a Table (continued)

do it!

8. Click  to apply the formula to the column and to close the dialog box. Click outside of the table to cancel the selection. The average of the values in the column, 5.04, now appears in the last cell of the table (see Figure 4-17).

9. Save and close the file with your changes.

more

Changing data in one of the cells that the calculation is based on does not immediately affect the result seen on the screen. To account for the new data and to update the calculation, select the column that has to be recalculated and press [F9], which is the Update Fields command.

When entering your own formulas into the Formula dialog box, you will reference other cells in the table using cell references. Cell references identify a cell's position by using a column letter and row number. For example, the cell reference for the third column, second row is C2 (see Figure 4-18). You can use the Word Formula feature in many ways. In Figure 4-19, formulas are used to calculate the total monthly spending for three people as well as the resulting 12-month projected total cost. The formulas shown are the ones that you would enter into the Formula text box when you called up the Formula dialog box with the insertion point in the appropriate cells. Each formula in the Monthly Total column (Column E) adds the numbers to the left in their respective rows to arrive at the total. Likewise, the formulas in the Annual Total column (Column F) multiply the monthly total from Column E by the 12 months in the year to arrive at a projected Annual Total.

Notice in Column F that the multiplication symbol is the asterisk (*), which is the uppercase symbol on the [8] key on the top row of your keyboard. The division symbol is a forward slash (/), the lowercase symbol near the lower right of your keyboard on the same key as the question mark. After you have entered data and formulas and have achieved a mathematical result, you can format the results by using the Number Format box in the Formula dialog box. In Figure 4-19, for example, we would recommend that you choose the $#,##0.00;($#,##0.00) format from the drop-down list. This format would place a dollar sign at the left edge of a result, place any needed commas in the thousands separator, provide a decimal place and two places to the right of the decimal, and place any negative results in parentheses.

Figure 4-17 lee-3.doc after calculating formula with dialog box

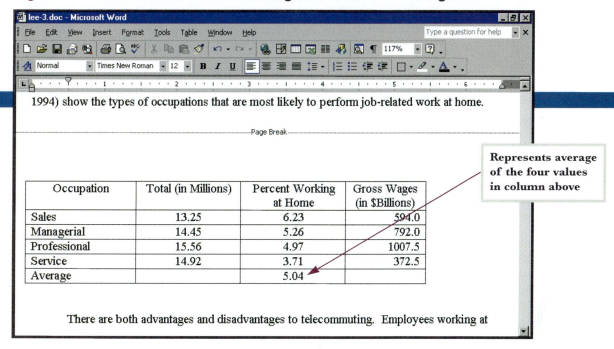

Figure 4-18 Cell References

Figure 4-19 Sample table with formulas

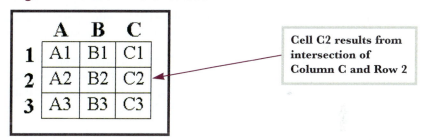

Practice

To practice calculating data in a table, open the Student File wdprac4-5.doc. Save and close any changes you make in your Word Files folder as mywdprac4-5.doc.

skill Formatting a Table

concept

You can change a table's appearance in many ways. Word's table formatting options include, among others, shading, borders, and 3-D effects. You can format individual table elements or apply an entire set of formatting changes to a table. Both techniques can improve the organization, clarity, and appearance of tables while saving you time when trying to create attractive and readable documents.

do it!

Format a table manually and with the Table AutoFormat command to improve its appearance.

1. Open Student File wddoit4-6.doc and save it in your Word Files folder as lee-4.doc. Scroll down to make the table visible. If necessary, turn on the Show/ Hide Paragraph button ¶. Notice that none of the headings contain hard returns (which would be indicated by a paragraph mark ¶), even though the headings in Columns C and D appear on two lines.

2. In Column A place the insertion point immediately to the left of the heading Occupation and press [Enter]. This action moves the word onto the second line of the cell.

3. In Column B place the insertion point immediately to the left of the opening parenthesis at the left of the word in, press [Backspace], and press [Enter]. This action eliminates the space, inserts a hard return, and moves the last two words with their parentheses to the second line of the heading.

4. In Column C click immediately to the left of the word at, press [Backspace], and press [Enter]. This action eliminates the space, inserts a hard return, and moves the last two words to the second line of the heading.

5. In Column D click immediately to the left of the opening parenthesis at the left of the word in, press [Backspace], and press [Enter]. This action eliminates the space inserts a hard return, and moves the last two words onto the second line of the heading. Turn off the Show/Hide Paragraph button.

6. With the insertion point still in the table, click Table, then click Table AutoFormat to open the Table AutoFormat dialog box. In the Table styles section, scroll down in the listings and click Table Grid 8. Be sure that check marks appear in all of the check boxes in the Apply special formats to section. The Preview section of the dialog box shows you what the formatted table will look like, depending on which table style you have clicked and which special formats have check marks.

7. Verify that your Table style and special formats conform to those in Figure 4-20. Then click Apply to apply the Grid 8 formatting and to close the dialog box.

8. Click Table, then click Table Properties to open the Table Properties dialog box. If necessary, click the Table tab to display it at the front of the dialog box. In the Alignment section, click Center, and then click OK to center the table horizontally on the page and to close the dialog box. Click anywhere outside of the table. Verify that the table format resembles that in Figure 4-21. If the format does not, make formatting adjustments as necessary to conform with the figure.

9. Save and close your document with the formatting changes you have made.

more If the top row of your table contains a heading and the table spans more than one page, you generally should display that heading at the top of each page where the table appears. To do so, place the insertion point anywhere in the top row, click Table, and then click Heading Rows Repeat. (Or access this command from the Row tab in the Table Properties dialog box.) You also should ensure that all lines of text and/or data in any given table row stay together in that row if the table spans more than one page. To prevent text and data from breaking across two pages, click Table, click Table Properties to open the Table Properties dialog box, click the Row tab to display it at the front of the dialog box, remove the check mark from the Allow row to break across pages check box, and click OK.

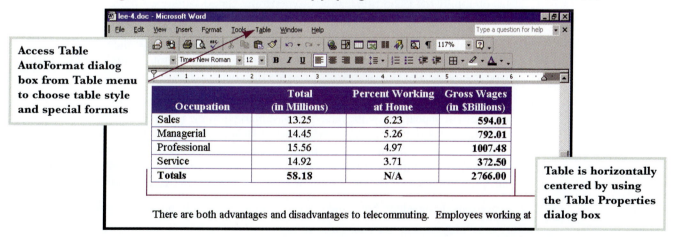

Figure 4-20 Table AutoFormat dialog box

- Click here to select which category of styles to display in Table styles box
- Scroll through list of table styles and click desired style
- Displays what selected table style will look like
- Turns formatting of selected parts of table on or off
- Opens New Style dialog box to create new table style
- Applies and saves any changes you made and closes dialog box

Figure 4-21 lee-4.doc after applying manual and automatic formats

- Access Table AutoFormat dialog box from Table menu to choose table style and special formats
- Table is horizontally centered by using the Table Properties dialog box

Practice

To practice formatting a table, open the Student File wdprac4-6.doc. Save and close any changes you make in your Word Files folder as mywdprac4-6.doc.

skill Creating a Chart

concept

Sometimes, readers will more readily understand a table if you present it as a chart. A chart not only represents data graphically instead of textually but also can provide an effective way to break up the monotony of line after line of text. Depending on your preference and the needs of the document that you are preparing, you can accompany the table with a chart or use the chart to completely replace the table. Word enables you to create a chart from scratch or, as you will do in this Skill, generate the chart from a pre-existing table.

do it!

Display a pre-existing table as a chart.

1. Open Student File wddoit4-7.doc and save it in your Word Files folder as lee-5.doc. Scroll to the table between the second and third paragraphs and click anywhere within it. In the bottom cell of the Percent Working at Home column, delete the letters N/A, which stand for Not Applicable, and which would frustrate your efforts to use the table-to-chart conversion subprogram.

2. Click Table, click Select, and click Table to select the entire table. Click Insert, and click Object. After a brief delay the Object dialog box opens with the Create New tab displayed.

3. Scroll down through the Object type box and double-click Microsoft Graph Chart. When this feature opens, it turns your table into a Microsoft Graph Datasheet (see Figure 4-22). A preliminary chart appears, based on the data in the table that you selected in Step 2.

4. Click Chart, then click Chart Options. The Chart Options dialog box opens with the Titles tab on top. In the Chart title text box, type Home-Based Workers. After a brief delay the title will appear at the top of the preview chart.

5. Press [Tab] to move the insertion point to the Category (X) text box, then type Occupation. After a brief delay the word will appear at the bottom of the preview chart (see Figure 4-23). Click [OK] to create the chart.

6. Click the Close Window button ⊠ to close the Datasheet window. The chart you have created will appear below the table in a hashmarked frame (see Figure 4-24). Some parts of the chart, especially the labels beneath it, will appear cramped and cut off. Notice that when the chart is selected, positioning the mouse pointer over a chart elements displays a ScreenTip displaying what part of the chart the element represents. Do not worry about the format, as you will learn how to modify a chart in the next Skill.

7. Click outside the chart. Save and close your document with the changes you have made.

more

The Chart Type dialog box, accessed from the Chart menu, offers 14 Standard chart types for representing data. Some of the more common chart types are the column chart, line chart, pie chart, and stock chart. Each Standard chart type offers two or more subtypes to choose from to increase your chart formatting options. On the Standard Types tab of the dialog box, you can click on the Press and Hold to View Sample button to see what your selected chart type will look like when you close the dialog box. The Custom Types tab of the dialog box offers 20 additional chart types and a preview area that displays what your selected custom chart type will look like.

Microsoft Graph automatically suggests the type of graph or chart Tbat seems to match most closely the format of your data, since not all formats properly represent all types of data. For example, you could not represent properly the table in this Skill with a pie-chart or radar graph. Therefore, when choosing a chart type, first determine which type will best represent your data.

Figure 4-22 Chart datasheet created from table

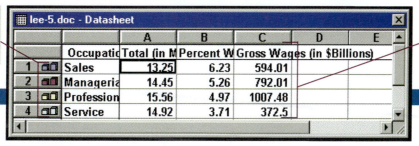

Shows the color used for each data series in chart

Headings and data in chart come from selected table

Figure 4-23 Chart Options dialog box

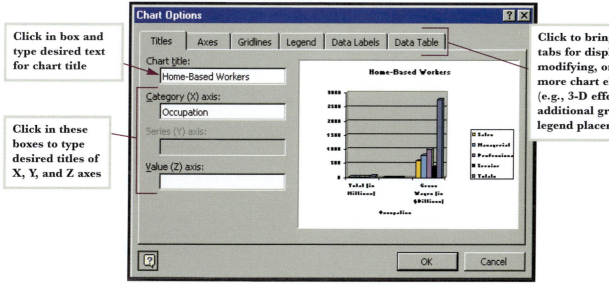

Click in box and type desired text for chart title

Click in these boxes to type desired titles of X, Y, and Z axes

Click to bring forward tabs for displaying, modifying, or hiding more chart elements (e.g., 3-D effects, additional gridlines, legend placement)

Figure 4-24 Chart created from table

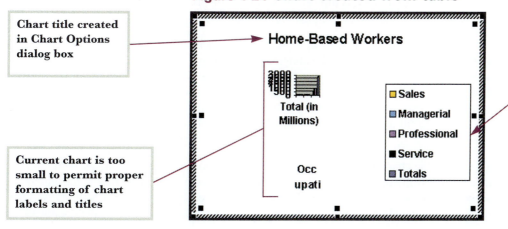

Chart title created in Chart Options dialog box

Current chart is too small to permit proper formatting of chart labels and titles

Legend identifies categories that appear in chart and shows colors that correspond with those in the datasheet

Practice

To practice creating a chart, open the Student File wdprac4-7.doc. Save and close any changes you make in your Word Files folder as mywdprac4-7.doc.

skill Editing a Chart

concept

Word treats charts as graphic objects instead of as text, but you still can modify charts by accessing the program that created them. You can edit virtually all aspects of a chart, including its size, position, and the characteristics of each element. Proper editing not only fixes formatting problems that exist when you first create a chart, but also offers the chance to add or delete data as needed and represent data in the most graphically pleasing and informative way.

do it !

Modify the appearance of a chart, especially its size, number of columns, and column labels.

1. Open Student File wddoit4-8.doc and save it as lee-6.doc. To see a more accurate image of how the finished chart eventually will look in your document, switch to Print Layout view.

2. Scroll down to the chart in the document, and double-click the chart to open Microsoft Graph. The Microsoft Graph toolbar will replace the Standard and Formatting toolbars at the top of the screen, and a hashmarked frame will appear around the chart with sizing handles at its corners and at the midpoint of each side. If necessary, drag the Datasheet window out of the way of the column chart (see Figure 4-25).

3. Click the midpoint sizing handle on the bottom of the chart's frame, drag it downward, and release it just below the 4½-inch mark on the Vertical Ruler. The chart expands vertically, making it possible for more increments to appear along the vertical axis of the chart.

4. Click the midpoint sizing handle on the right side of the frame, drag it to the right, and release it when it is even with the 5½-inch mark on the Horizontal Ruler. The chart expands horizontally until it is almost the width of the body text and has room to display the column labels along the bottom axis of the chart without breaking them awkwardly.

5. In the Datasheet window click the gray header for column C (Gross Wages in $Billions), and press [Delete] to remove the heading and data for that column. Also in the Datasheet window, click the gray header for row 5 (Totals) and press [Delete] to remove the heading and data for that row. The chart columns associated with column C and for row 5 disappear from the chart, and the remaining columns (Total in Millions and Percent Working at Home) widen to fill the chart background. The Totals reference in the chart Legend also disappears.

6. Click outside the chart frame to return to the regular Word document window with the Standard and Formatting toolbars. Because you deleted column C and row 5, the edited chart now displays only the columns for the remaining categories Total in Millions and the Percent Working at Home (see Figure 4-26). Save your changes and close the document.

more

When working with a chart in Word, remember that the chart is a foreign element created by another application. To edit the chart itself, you first must double-click it to open its parent application. To edit a chart based on changed table data, you either must alter the datasheet for the table—available on the View menu of the Graph program—or recreate the chart. To act upon the chart as an element of your Word document (e.g., move or copy it), click it only once to select it. A box indicated by sizing handles—not the hashmarked frame indicating the parent application—will appear around it. You then may cut and paste the chart or drag and drop it to another place in the document. You also can change text added during chart creation, such as title and category, by selecting the specific element and entering new text. When you select a chart element like the title, a frame will appear around it, letting you know you may edit it.

Figure 4-25 Unedited chart displayed in MS Graph application

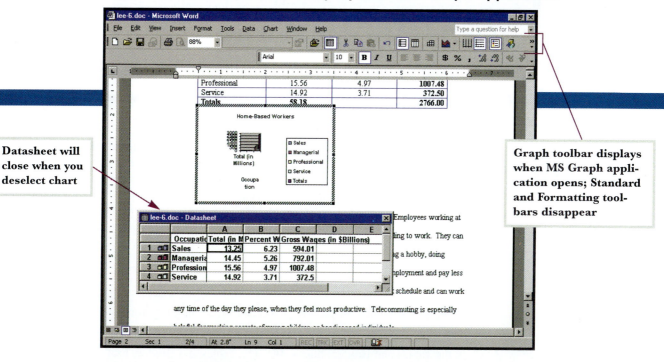

Figure 4-26 Edited chart displayed in Print Layout view

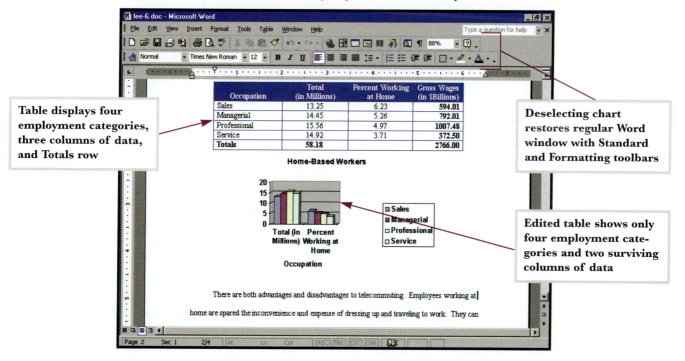

Practice

To practice editing a chart, open Student File **wdprac4-8.doc**. Save and close any changes you make in your Word Files folder as **mywdprac4-8.doc**.

skill: Drawing a Table

concept

As earlier Skills show, Word enables you to create tables with predefined borders using the Insert Table button. However, you sometimes may want to have more control over the construction of a table. Work makes this possible by letting you draw a table gridline by gridline with the Draw Table tool. With this tool you can create a table customized precisely for your needs as easily as you can create a standard table. Drawn tables still allow you to merge or split cells, change column widths, and make other edits common to standard tables.

do it!

Draw a table, merge the top row, and enter text in all of the cells.

1. Click ⬜ to open a new blank document, and save it in your Word Files folder as progress.doc.

2. Click the Tables and Borders button ⬜. The Tables and Borders toolbar will appear, floating on the screen. If the toolbar obscures your document window, drag it by its title bar to a better location—such as directly underneath the Formatting toolbar where it will be docked out of the way. The document now should be in Print Layout view.

3. Type Progress Table on the first line of the document, and press [Enter].

4. On the Tables and Borders toolbar, click the Draw Table button ⬜. The mouse pointer now should look like a pencil when it is over the document. The Draw Table button is the first button on the Tables and Borders toolbar. Be careful not to confuse it with the Border Color button, which looks similar but has a thick line below the pencil icon.

5. Position the mouse pointer just below the word Progress. Hold down the mouse button and drag from that point down and to the right. As you drag, a dashed outline of a table will appear. Release the mouse button when the outline reaches 4 inches on the Horizontal Ruler and 3 inches on the Vertical Ruler (see Figure 4-27).

6. Place the mouse pointer on the top border of the table at the 2-inch mark on the Horizontal Ruler. Click and drag straight down to the bottom border, drawing a vertical line in the middle of the table.

7. Place the mouse pointer on the left border of the table at the ½-inch mark on the Vertical Ruler. Click and drag straight across to the right border, drawing a horizontal line.

8. Repeat the previous step to create four more horizontal lines every ½-inch down the Vertical Ruler. Verify that your table now resembles Figure 4-28. If it does not, click the Undo button ⬜ until you reach an earlier stage of the table that matches the Steps listed above.

9. Click ⬜ to turn off the Draw Table tool. Resave the document with the changes you have made thus far, but do **not** close the file.

(continued on WD 4.24)

Figure 4-27 Table border drawn by hand

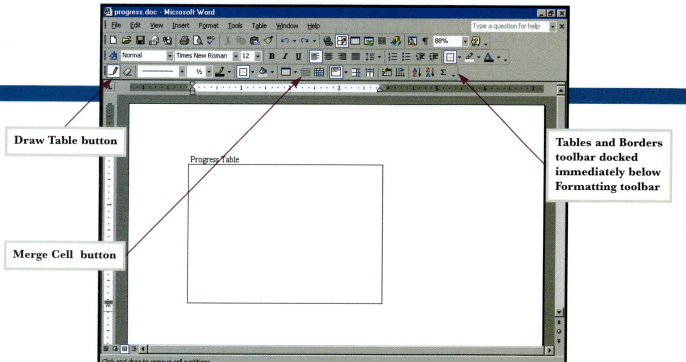

Figure 4-28 Table with drawn gridlines

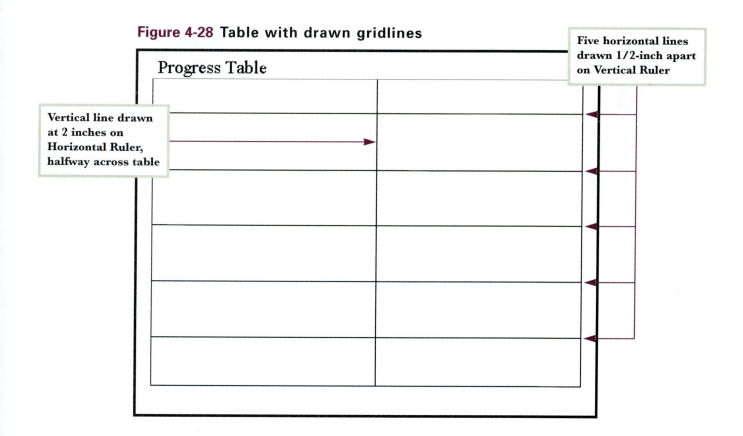

skill Drawing a Table (continued)

do it!

10. Highlight the entire line of text above the table, cut it, and paste it into cell A1.

11. Click in the Selection bar to the left of Row A to select cells A1 and B1. On the Tables and Borders toolbar, click the Merge Cells button. Cells A1 and B1 are combined into one cell.

12. With the merged cell still selected, click the Bold button on the Formatting toolbar. The text in the selected cell is bolded.

13. Click in cell A2 to place the insertion point there and to deselect cell A1 (see Figure 4-29). In cell A2, type the word Task.

14. Press [Tab] to move the insertion point to cell B2. In cell B2 type the words Deadline. Use the Selection bar to highlight row 2 of the table, and then click the Underline button. A line is placed beneath all text in the row.

15. Consult Figure 4-30, and type the text that appears there into the corresponding cells in your table.

16. Save and close your document with the changes you have made.

more

You can activate the Draw Table tool at any time to add more gridlines to a table. You also can remove gridlines, thereby eliminating rows and/or columns, by clicking the Eraser button on the Tables and Borders toolbar. Simply click on a gridline with the eraser to remove the line.

As you have seen, you can apply font formats to text in a table just as you would in a normal document. Most formatting options that you have applied to text in other Skills are available in tables too, including alignment, font style, font size, and font color. You even can rotate text in a cell by clicking the Text Direction button on the Tables and Borders toolbar.

Figure 4-29 Merged cell with bold font applied

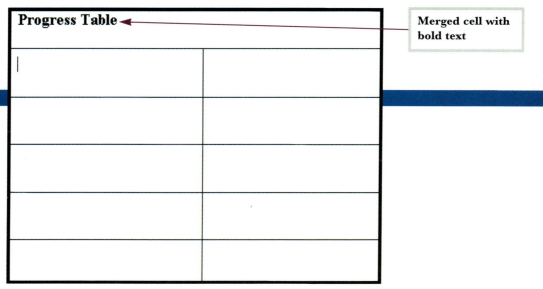

Figure 4-30 Drawn table with entered text

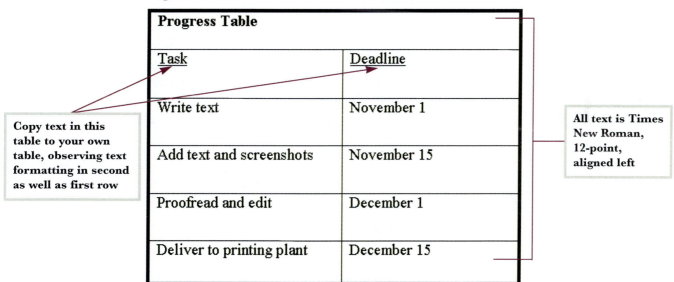

Practice

Use the Draw Table tool to create a table that will enable you to plot statistics from a survey in which people were asked to name their favorite season. Save and close this table in your Word Files folder as mywdprac4-9.doc.

skill — Adding Borders and Shading

concept

An earlier Skill in this Lesson teaches how to enhance the appearance of a table using the AutoFormat command from the Table menu. This command enables you to apply a predetermined set of formats to a table. Although AutoFormat does offer some options, it does not permit as many formatting changes as some people might like. Just as the Draw Table command gives you greater control over structuring a table, so also the Table Properties command provides many options for enhancing the appearance of a table.

do it!

Add a customized border and shading to a table.

1. Open Student File wddoit4-9.doc and save it in your Word Files folder as progress1.doc.

2. Click Table, click Select, and then click Table on the submenu. The entire table will be selected.

3. Click Table again, then click Table Properties. The Table Properties dialog box will open to the Table tab.

4. At the bottom center of the tab, click the Borders and Shading button [Borders and Shading...]. The Borders and Shading dialog box opens to the Borders tab.

5. In the Setting section of the tab, click the All option. In the Style box, click the third option, which looks like tightly spaced dashes.

6. At the right edge of the Color box, click the drop-down arrow to open a color palette. Then click the Blue square, which is the sixth square in the second row.

7. At the right edge of the Width box, click the drop-down arrow to open a list of line weights, or thicknesses. Then select the 2 1/4 pt option.

8. Look at the Preview diagram near the upper right area of the Borders tab. Verify that the border formats that you have selected match those that appear in Figure 4-31. If your Preview diagram does not match the figure, review the Steps above and make the needed changes.

9. Click [OK] to accept the formatting choices and to close the Borders and Shading dialog box. Click [OK] again to close the Table Properties dialog box.

10. Click outside of the modified table to deselect it. Verify that it now looks like Figure 4-32. Save your document with the changes you have made thus far, but do **not** close the file.

(continued on WD 4.28)

Figure 4-31 Border tab of Borders and Shading dialog box

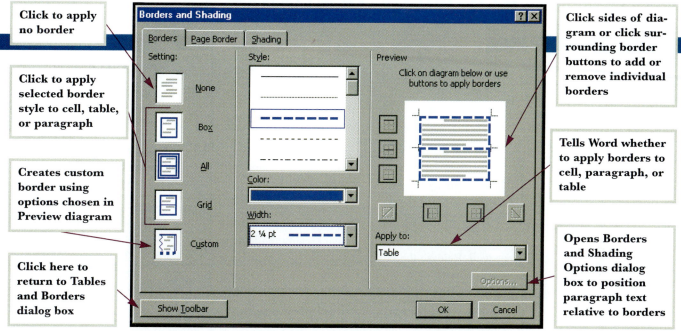

Figure 4-32 Drawn table with applied border

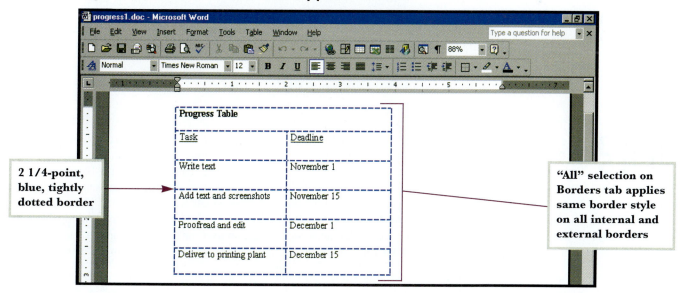

skill   Adding Borders and Shading (continued)

do it!

11. Click inside of cell A1 to activate it. If necessary, click the Tables and Borders button on the Standard toolbar to display the Tables and Borders toolbar.

12. On the Tables and Borders toolbar, click the arrow on the right edge of the Shading Color button. The Shading Color palette will appear. Click the Gray-25% option, which is the seventh square in the first row of the palette (see Figure 4-33). Word shades the active cell with the color you have selected.

13. Click in the Selection bar immediately to the left of row 2 of the table to select the entire row. Hold down the [Ctrl] key and, using the Selection bar again, highlight rows 4 and 6 as well. Release the [Ctrl] key. As a new feature in Word 2002, you can select non-adjacent areas of a document—for example, the first and fourth paragraphs of a text document or (as in this Step) the second, fourth, and sixth rows of the table. After selecting these areas, you then can format them alike.

14. Click the arrow on the right edge of the Shading Color button to display the Shading Color palette again. Click the Pale Blue option, which is the sixth square in the bottom row (see Figure 4-34). Word shades the second, fourth, and sixth rows with the color you have selected. You may apply the current Shading Color multiple times by clicking the Shading Color button itself rather than clicking the arrow next to it.

15. Click outside of the table to cancel the selection. Verify that the format of your table now matches that of Figure 4-35. If your table does not, click the Undo button as many times as needed to clear the mistaken formats, review the Steps you missed, and redo them.

16. Save and close your document with the changes you have made.

more   Figure 4-31 shows that the Borders and Shading dialog box contains not only a Borders tab but also a Page Borders and Shading tab. The Box, Shadow, 3-D, and Custom options apply formats around a whole page just as the same boxes on the Borders tab do so for tables. These four options on the Page Borders tab also resemble their counterparts on the Borders tab in that they apply formats according to the current settings in the Style, Color, and Width boxes. However, the Page Borders tab also has an Art box that offers small graphics to use in place of lined, dotted, and other borders in the Style box. The Preview diagram on the Page Borders tab works like the corresponding diagram on the Borders tab. You can apply borders by clicking the border areas on the diagram itself or the border buttons surrounding the diagram. The Page Borders tab also contains a Show Toolbar and an Options button for further formatting effects.

The Shading tab of the Borders and Shading dialog box offers fewer formatting options than do the other two tabs but it still helps you produce attractive formatting effects. Like the Shading Color button on the Tables and Borders toolbar, the Shading tab offers a color palette of over fifty colors and shades of gray to provide fill colors for rows and columns. A More Colors button opens the same Colors dialog box that the More Fill Colors area of the Shading Color button does. The Patterns section of the Shading tab contains a Style box that enables you to apply shaded or patterned colors over the top of the fill colors and a Colors box to dictate which colors will appear in those shaded or patterned areas. Lastly, the Shading tab also has a Preview area that shows what your formatting results will be and an Apply to box that dictates what precise area the Shading selection will affect.

Figure 4-33 Shading Color palette with Gray-25% option

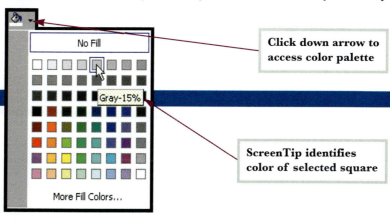

Figure 4-34 Shading Color palette with Pale Blue option

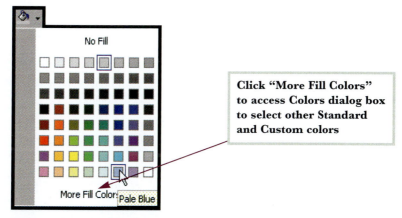

Figure 4-35 Table formatted with all desired borders and shading

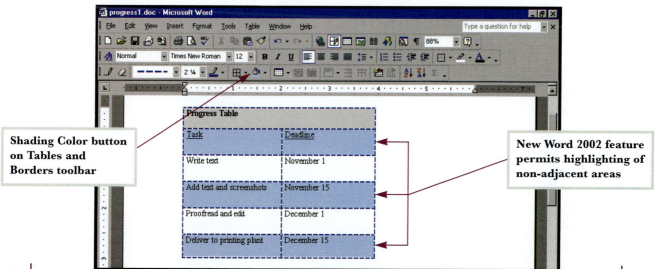

Practice

To practice formatting a table with borders and shading, reopen Student File mywdprac4-6.doc. Change the alternating shaded rows to light green, and the borders around the first and last rows to dashed lines. Save and close any changes in your Word Files folder as mywdprac4-10.doc.

shortcuts

Function	Button/Mouse	Menu	Keyboard
Insert a table		Click Table, click Insert, click Table	
Insert a row above the selected row	Right-click to the left of selected row, then click Insert Rows	Click Table, click Insert, click Rows Above	
Insert a row below the selected row		Click Table, click Insert, click Rows Below	
Insert a column to the left of the selected column	Right-click above selected column, then click Insert Columns	Click Table, click Insert, click Columns to the Left	
Insert a column to the right of the selected column		Click Table, click Insert, click Columns to the Right	
Select entire table	Click Table Move handle (Print Layout View)	Click Table, highlight Select, then click Table	
Delete the selected table		Click Table, click Delete, click Table	
Delete the selected row	Right-click to the left of the selected row, then click Delete Rows	Click Table, click Delete, click Rows	[Shift]+[Delete]
Delete the selected column	Right-click above the selected column, then click Delete Columns	Click Table, click Delete, click Columns	[Shift]+[Delete]
Align to the left selected text in a cell or a paragraph			[Ctrl]+[L]
Align to the right selected text in a cell or a paragraph			[Ctrl]+[R]
Center selected text in a cell or paragraph			[Ctrl]+[E]
Justify selected text in a cell or paragraph			[Ctrl]+[J]
Repeat last action		Click Edit, then click Repeat [action name]	[Ctrl]+[Y]

A. Identify Key Features

Name the items indicated by callouts in Figure 2-24.

Figure 4-36 Identifying components of a toolbar and a table

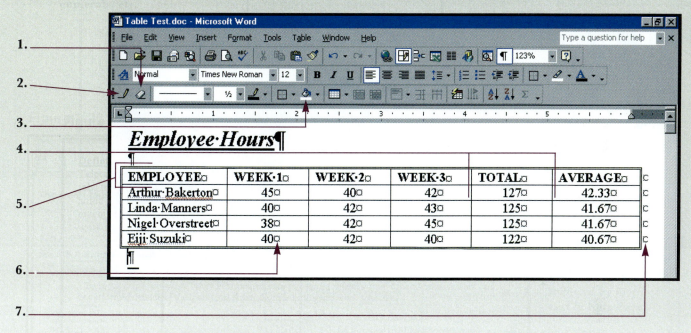

1.
2.
3.
4.
5.
6.
7.

B. Select the Best Answer

8. An order in which you can sort data
9. Explains the symbols and colors being used in a chart
10. The visible boundary between cells in a basic table
11. The intersection of a row and a column
12. An existing worksheet that becomes part of a Word document
13. A command list that appears when you right-click a table
14. A graphic representation of a table
15. A visual element indicating a selected chart
16. What Word uses to calculate data in a table

a. Chart
b. Table shortcut menu
c. Embedded object
d. Legend
e. Ascending
f. Formula
g. Gridline
h. Hatchmark
i. Cell

quiz (continued)

C. Complete the Statement

17. The Insert Table button:
    a. Creates a table based on the Normal template
    b. Creates a table based on dimensions you choose
    c. Pastes data from the Clipboard into a table
    d. Inserts a default table of 4 rows and 4 columns

18. To move the insertion point to the next cell of a table in the current row:
    a. Press [End]
    b. Press [Tab]
    c. Double-click the table
    d. Press [Shift]+[Enter]

19. D14 refers to:
    a. The fourteenth row in the fourth column
    b. The fourteenth column in the fourth row
    c. A formula with at least fourteen values
    d. A document designation for a Word table

20. The first step in creating a chart from a selected table is to:
    a. Click the chart button
    b. Press [Ctrl]+[F8]
    c. Click Insert, then click Chart
    d. Click Insert, then click Object

21. Paragraphs and table columns both have:
    a. Page numbers
    b. Selection bars
    c. Gridlines
    d. Cell markers

22. The Chart Legend:
    a. Summarizes a Chart Wizard's instructions
    b. Must be created in Excel and linked to Word
    c. Displays the Tables and Borders toolbar
    d. Explains the meaning of colors used in the chart

23. You may delete columns by accessing the:
    a. Table menu
    b. Tools menu
    c. Edit menu
    d. Format menu

24. You must use an equal sign before a formula or Word will:
    a. Use the wrong data to calculate the formula
    b. Use the correct data, but calculate incorrectly
    c. Calculate the last row of data by default
    d. Read the data as a label and not calculate anything

25. To sort data in a table you should:
    a. Open the Sort dialog box, and use it to sort the data
    b. Open the Sort data program in Excel or Access
    c. Open the Sort tool on the Edit menu
    d. Open the Sort menu and choose the Ascending or Descending command

26. The Borders and Shading dialog box contains all **but** the following:
    a. Border Design, Color, and Shading tabs
    b. A Setting section on the Borders tab
    c. A Style section on the Page Border tab
    d. A Preview area on the Shading tab

Build Your Skills

1. Open a new document, create a table, and add data to it:

   a. Open a new Word document and immediately save it as Employees.doc.

   b. Click Table, then click Insert Table to open the Insert Table dialog box. Create a table that is 5 columns by 4 rows and close the dialog box.

   c. Label the cells across the top row as follows: Name, March, April, May, and Average.

   d. Enter a first and a last name into each of the lower three cells in the leftmost column.

   e. Insert a number between 18 and 22 into each of the three cells to the right of each name, for a total of nine cells.

2. Average the columns and sort the table:

   a. Position the insertion point in the second cell down in the Average column, which is cell E2.

   b. Click Table, then click Formula to open the Formula dialog box. Enter the formula =AVERAGE(B2:D2) into the Formula text box, choose the Number format 0.00, and press [Enter].

   c. Repeat Steps a and b for the other two cells in the Average column, making sure that you use the correct cell references for the related calculation. Sort the table in the order of ascending average.

3. Format and resave the table:

   a. Place the insertion point anywhere inside the table, click Table, and then click Table AutoFormat. Select a simple Table Style that does not include any cell shading. In the Apply special formats to section, be sure that only the Heading rows and First column check boxes are checked, and press [Enter].

   b. Alter the existing formatting by shading the first row of the table with Gray-20% and bolding the heading text if needed. Also apply an All border with a Solid line, Dark Blue color, and 1-1/2 point width.

   c. Be sure the text in the Names column is aligned left and that the text in the other four columns is centered. Using the Table tab on the Table Properties dialog box, center the table horizontally on the page. Resave the table with the changes you have made thus far.

4. Create a chart from the existing table.

   a. Highlight only the first four columns of the table you created above. Click Insert, click Object, click the Create New tab if needed, click Microsoft Graph Chart, and then press [Enter] to create a chart and to close the dialog box.

   b. On the Titles tab of the Chart Options dialog box, type Monthly Workdays in the Chart title box. Type Month in the Category (X) axis box. Press [Enter] to confirm the titles and to close the dialog box.

   c. Close the Datasheet. Drag the right edge of the chart so it lines up with the decimal places in the last column of the table above it. Click outside the chart to verify that it is centered horizontally on the page. If you need to adjust the size and position of the chart, click on it only once, use the sizing handles to adjust it, and then deselect the chart.

   d. Resave and close the document with the changes you have made.

interactivity (continued)

Problem Solving Exercises

1. Create a table to display the high and low temperatures for each of the last five days (use fictional numbers if you do not have available data). Add two columns to the table to include the high and the low temperatures for the five-day period, and use the Formula dialog box to calculate the five-day averages. Then convert the table into a chart. Finally, add a row to the bottom of the table, merge the cells, and type your name. Save the file as Temperatures.doc.

2. Create a table to help calculate the grade-point averages of the students you have been tutoring for the last two years.

    a. Using the data below, calculate the Grade Point Average (GPA) for every student over the two-year period.

    b. Calculate the combined GPA of all the students for each semester that you tutored the students.

    c. Calculate the overall GPA, including every student, over the two-year period.

    d. Sort the table by the highest individual GPA, as found in question 2a, over the last two years.

    e. AutoFormat the table with a Colorful style, applying special formats to the heading row, the last row, and the first column. Make sure your name is included in the document, and save it as GPA.doc.

Student	Semester 1	Semester 2	Semester 3	Semester 4
Rosa	3.6	3.1	4.0	2.7
Zi	3.3	3.9	3.5	3.0
Donny	2.8	2.3	2.4	3.7
Melanie	3.1	1.4	2.9	2.5
Tsuyoshi	1.7	2.6	2.0	2.9

3. As the leader of a public relations team, you are responsible for your employees' business expenses. Create a table to calculate information about their expenses over the first half of the year. Format all dollar amounts with dollar signs and two decimal places. Use the Formula dialog box to calculate all totals and averages. (Hint: the table probably will fit best in Landscape page orientation).

    a. Using the data below, figure out the total each employee spent.

    b. Calculate the total that the entire team spent over the six-month period.

    c. Calculate the average amount per month spent by each employee over the six-month period.

    d. Calculate the average amount spent by the team every month.

    e. Use the default Chart type to create a chart representing the table you have created. Make any modifications to the chart that you feel are necessary to make it as informative, attractive, and readable as possible.

    f. Add your name to the document and save it as Expenses.doc.

Employees	Jan	Feb	Mar	Apr	May	Jun
Isa	113	158	306	400	322	150
Gao	150	150	258	350	300	125
Jill	200	320	354	410	300	100

a

Alignment
The position of text or objects in relation to the margins of a page. Word's horizontal alignment options for text are right, left, centered, and justified.

Answer Wizard
The Microsoft Word Help tab that allows you to ask questions just as you would ask the Office Assistant.

Application
See program.

Arrow keys
The [→], [←], [↑], and [↓] keys on the keyboard. Used to move the insertion point, select from a menu or a list of options, or in combination with other keys to execute specific commands such as selecting text.

Ascending order
See Sort order.

AutoFit
A feature that resizes table columns to match their contents or, on Web pages, resizes the entire table so that it fits on the visible page when the window is resized.

Automatic save
A feature that automatically saves document changes in a temporary file at specified intervals. If power to the computer is interrupted, the changes in effect from the last save are retained. Enabled by default, you can turn off this feature from the Save tab of the Options dialog box on the Tools menu.

AutoCorrect
A feature that automatically corrects misspelled words as they are entered. Word provides many entries for commonly misspelled words, but you may also add your own.

AutoFormat
A feature that improves the appearance of a document by applying consistent formatting and styles based on a default document template or a document template that you specify. The AutoFormat feature can also add bullets or numbers to lists and symbols for trademarks and copyrights where necessary.

AutoText
Text that Word is programmed to recognize. When you begin to type a word or phrase that Word recognizes, the program offers to complete it for you.

Axis
A horizontal or vertical line bordering a chart area providing a frame of reference for measuring the chart's data; the horizontal line is the X axis, and the vertical line is the Y axis.

b

Blank Document template
The collection of settings used in the blank document you see when you first launch Word or when you click the New button on the Standard toolbar.

Break
A feature that ends a current line, section, or page of text and/or graphics and starts the material on the next line, section, or page.

Browser
An application that allows you to find and view information on the World Wide Web. Major browsers include Netscape Navigator and Microsoft Internet Explorer.

Bullet
A character or symbol, often a heavy dot, used to separate items in a list.

c

Case
Refers to whether or not a letter is capitalized. Some search features are case-sensitive; that is, they will differentiate between words that are spelled the same but have different capitalization.

Cell
The basic unit of a table, separated by gridlines. In a table, the intersection of a row and a column forms one cell.

Cell reference
A code that identifies a cell's position in a table. Each cell reference contains a letter indicating its column and a number indicating its row.

Character style
A combination of character formats from the Font dialog box that is identified by a style name. Changing an element (such as the font size) of a character style changes all text that has been formatted with that style.

Chart
A graphical representation of data.

Click
To press and release a mouse button in one motion; usually refers to the left mouse button.

Click and drag
To press and hold the mouse button, move the mouse along a flat surface, and then release the mouse button at the appropriate time.

Clip art
A precreated, usually copyright-free, graphic image that can be inserted into a document to illustrate a point or to add visual interest. Clip art often comes in large collections.

Clip Gallery
A Microsoft Office feature that acts as a library of clip art, pictures, sounds and videos. It allows you to import, store, and reuse these objects in Word documents and in other Office applications.

Clipboard
A temporary storage area for cut or copied text or graphics. You can paste the contents of the Clipboard into any Word document or into a file of another Microsoft Windows program. The Office Clipboard differs from the Windows Clipboard in that it can hold up to 24 items at once. You can view the contents of the Office Clipboard by activating the Clipboard Task Pane from the Edit menu.

Column
In documents, a vertically arranged section of text and/or graphics on a page; in tables, a vertically arranged collection of cells and generally containing the same category of information.

Contents tab
The Microsoft Word Help tab that organizes Help topics like a table of contents or outline.

Control menu
Menu available from the Title bar that contains commands for managing the active window.

Copy
To send a copy of selected text or a graphic from a document to the Clipboard so that you may be reproduce it elsewhere in the document or in another document.

Custom dictionary
A document containing all the words that have been "learned" by Word's spell checker. More that one custom dictionary can be created and referenced by a single copy of Microsoft Word.

Cut
To remove selected text or a graphic from a document to the Clipboard so that it may be reinserted elsewhere in the document or in another document.

Datasheet
A grid of data related to a chart that has been created from a pre-existing table.

Defaults
Predefined settings for variable items such as page margins, tab spacing, and shortcut key assignments; these can be changed when necessary.

Descending order
See Sort order.

Destination file
The file to which you transfer a source file—for example, a business report in Word that uses a table from another program like Excel or Access.

Dialog box
A box that displays the available command options for you to review or change before executing a command.

Document window
The window on the screen in which a document is viewed and edited. When the document window is maximized, it shares its borders and title bar with the Word application window.

Double-click
To press and release a mouse button twice rapidly; usually refers to the left mouse button.

Drag
To hold down the mouse button while moving the mouse.

Drag-and-drop
Method of moving selected text and objects by dragging them from one location to another with the mouse.

Draw Table tool
Allows you to create the borders and gridlines of a table freehand.

Drive
The mechanism in a computer that reads recordable media (such as a disk or tape cartridge) to retrieve and store information. Personal computers often have one hard disk drive labeled C, a drive that reads floppy disks labeled A, and a drive that reads CDs labeled D.

Edit
To add, delete, or modify text or other elements of a file.

Effects
Text formats such as small caps, all caps, hidden text, strikethrough, subscript, or superscript.

Embedded object
Information contained in a source file and inserted in a destination file; after embedding, the object becomes part of the destination file; changes made in the embedded object are reflected in only the destination file (see also Linked object).

Endnote
Explanatory material, usually marked by a sequential number or letter, that appears at the end of a document (see Footnote).

Extend selection
To increase the selected area. When a selection is extended, it grows progressively larger each time [F8] is pressed. To shrink the selection, press [Shift]+[F8]. The arrow keys may also be used with the [Shift] key to enlarge or shrink the selection.

Field
The place in a main document where a specific portion of a record, such as a postal code, will be inserted when the document is merged. Also known as a merge field.

File
A document that has been created and saved under a unique file name. In Word, all documents and pictures are stored as files (see also Destination file, Source file).

Find and Replace
To search for text or graphics in a document and then to substitute other text or graphics in its place.

Folders
Subdivisions of a disk that work like a filing system to help you organize files.

Font
A name given to a collection of text characters at a certain size, weight, and style. Font has become synonymous with typeface. Arial and Times New Roman are examples of font names.

Font size
Refers to the physical size of text, measured in points (pts). The more points, the larger the appearance of the text on the page.

Font style
Refers to whether text appears as bold, italicized, or underlined, or any combination of these formats.

Footnote
Explanatory material, usually marked by a sequential number or letter, that appears at the bottom, or "foot," of a document; a footnote usually comments or expands upon the main text to which it refers (see Endnote).

Format
The way text appears on a page. In Word, formats come from direct formatting or the application of styles. The four formatting levels are character, paragraph, section, and document.

Format Painter
A tool enabling you to copy many formatting settings from selected text to another section of text; it is especially useful in documents like flyers and newsletters where distinctive formatting is common, even essential, to the document's appearance.

Formula
A mathematical expression that performs a calculation in a table.

Global template
In Word, a template named NORMAL.DOT that contains default menus, AutoCorrect entries, styles and page setup settings. Documents use the global template unless a custom template is specified. See also template.

Gridlines
The lines that separate cells in a table. Gridlines do not print. You can alternately hide and display gridlines with the Gridlines command on the Table menu.

Hanging indent
A paragraph format in which the first line of a paragraph extends farther to the left than subsequent lines.

Header/footer
A header is an item or group of items that appears at the top of every page in a section. A footer appears at the bottom of every page. Headers and footers often contain page numbers, chapter titles, dates, and author names.

Hidden text
A character format that allows you to show or hide designated text. Word indicates hidden text by underlining it with a dotted line. You can select or clear the Hidden Text option with the Options command on the Tools menu. Hidden text may be omitted when printing.

Horizontal ruler
A bar displayed across the top of the document window in all views. The ruler can be used to indent paragraphs, set tab stops, adjust left and right paragraph margins, and change column widths in a table. You can hide this ruler by clicking View, then clicking Ruler.

HTML
An acronym for HyperText Markup Language, which is the language that defines the way information is presented on a Web page. Word can automatically convert the formatting you have given a document into HTML, which functionally turns your document into a Web page.

HTTP
An acronym for HyperText Transfer Protocol; appears at the beginning of a URL to notify the browser that the following information is a hypertext Web document.

Hyperlink
Originated as an element of Web page design; usually text, clicking a hyperlink brings you directly to a predefined location within a document or to a specific page on the World Wide Web.

Indent
The distance between text boundaries and page margins. Positive indents make the text area narrower than the space between margins. Negative indents allow text to extend into the margins. A paragraph can have left, right, and first-line indents.

Index tab
The Microsoft Word Help tab that allows you to query the Help files using an alphabetical list of keywords.

Insertion point
A vertical blinking line on the Word screen that indicates where text and graphics will be inserted. The insertion point also determines where Word will begin an action.

l

Label
In tables, data consisting of words (see also Value); in printing, a small, generally rectangular, adhesive-backed sheet of paper for printing folder captions, addresses, or similar data for mass printing

Landscape
A term used to refer to horizontal page orientation; opposite of "portrait," or vertical, orientation.

Line break
A mark inserted where you want to end one line and start another without starting a new paragraph. A line break may be inserted by pressing [Shift]+[Return].

Line spacing
The height of a line of text, often measured in lines or points.

Linked object
Information contained in a source file and inserted in a destination file that maintains a connection between the two files; after embedding, changes made in the source file object can be reflected in the destination file (see also Embedded object).

m

Margin
The distance between the edge of the text in the document and the top, bottom, or side edges of the page.

Maximize
To enlarge a window to its maximum size. Maximizing an application window causes it to fill the screen; maximizing a document window causes it to fill the application window.

Menu bar
Lists the names of menus containing Word commands. Click a menu name on the Menu bar to display a list of commands.

Merge cells
Command that combines two or more cells in a table into one cell.

Microsoft Graph Chart
A program that displays a chart created from a pre-existing table and a datasheet containing data related to the chart; you can directly access the the chart and datasheet to change their contents and/or appearance.

Minimize
To shrink a window to its minimum size. Minimizing a window reduces it to a button on the Windows taskbar.

My Computer
A Windows operating system utility that gives you access to the various disk drives and other resources available to your computer.

Nonprinting characters
Marks displayed on the screen to indicate characters that do not print, such as paragraph marks or spaces. You can control the display of these characters with the Options command on the Tools menu, and the Show/Hide ¶ button on the Standard toolbar.

Normal View
Used for most editing and formatting tasks. Normal View shows text formatting but simplifies the layout of the page so that you can type and edit quickly.

Note pane
A special window in which the text of all the footnotes in a document appears. The note pane can be accessed by double-clicking a note reference mark.

Object
A table, chart, graphic, equation, or other form of information you create and edit with a program other than Word, but whose data you insert and store in a Word document.

Office Assistant
An animated manifestation of the Microsoft Office help facility. The Office Assistant provides hints, instructions, and a convenient interface between the user and Word's various Help features.

Options
The choices available in a dialog box.

Overtype
An option for replacing existing characters one by one as you type. You can select overtype by selecting the Overtype option on the Edit tab with the Options command on the Tools menu. When you select the Overtype option, the letters "OVR" appear in the status bar at the bottom of the Word window. You can also double-click these letters in the status bar to activate or deactivate overtype mode.

Page Break
The point at which one page ends and another begins. A break you insert is called a hard break; a break determined by the page layout is called a soft break. In Normal View, a hard break appears as a dotted line and is labeled Page Break, while a soft break appears as a dotted line without a label.

Paragraph style
A stored set of paragraph format settings.

Paste
To insert cut or copied text or objects into a document from the Clipboard.

Paste Options button
Appears when you execute the Paste command. Clicking the Paste Options button opens a menu of commands that allows you to determine what formatting will be used on the item you pasted.

Path
The address of a file's location. It contains the drive, folder and subfolders, and file name. For example, the complete path for Microsoft Word might be C:\Program Files\Microsoft Office\Winword.exe.

Point size
A measurement used for the size of type characters. There are 72 points per inch.

Portrait
A term used to refer to vertical page orientation; opposite of "landscape," or horizontal, orientation.

Position
The specific placement of graphics, tables, and paragraphs on a page. In Word, you can assign items to fixed positions on a page.

Preview Area
A section of a dialog box that displays the results of formatting using the current settings of the dialog box.

Preview Diagram
A section of a dialog box that displays the results of formatting using the current settings of the dialog box and has additional tools surrounding the display to alter formatting.

Print Layout View
A view of a document as it will appear when you print it. Items such as headers, footnotes, and framed objects appear in their actual positions, and you can drag them to new positions.

Print Preview
Allows you to view a document as it will appear when printed. Includes a Magnifier tool, a text-editing tool, and the ability to view multiple pages at once.

Program
A software application that performs specific tasks, such as Microsoft Word or Microsoft Excel.

Program window
A window that contains the running program. The window displays the menus and provides the workspace for any document used within the application. The application window shares its borders and title bar with maximized document windows.

Read-Only
A file setting that allows a file to be opened and read, but not modified.

Redo
Counteracts the Undo command by repeating previously reversed actions or changes, usually editing or formatting commands. Only actions that have been undone can be reversed with the redo command.

Repeat
Command that performs your most recent operation again.

Resize
To change the size of an object (such as framed text or a graphic) by dragging sizing handles located on the sides and corner of the selected object, or by adjusting its dimensions in a dialog box.

Restore
To reduce a window to its size before it was maximized.

Right-click
To click the right mouse button; often necessary to access specialized menus and shortcuts. The designated right and left mouse buttons may be reversed with the Mouse control panel to accommodate user preferences.

Row
In tables, a horizontally arranged collection of cells generally containing various categories of information related to a particular person, place, type of data, or topic.

Ruler
A horizontal or vertical bar marked with measurements such as inches or centimeters that displays, respectively, at the top or left edge of a document window.

Sans serif font
A font whose characters do not include serifs, the small strokes at the ends of the characters. Arial and Helvetica are sans serif fonts.

Save
To store a computer file electronically on a device such as a floppy disk or hard drive so that you can retrieve the file even after you have shut down the computer.

Save As
Command you use to save a new file for the first time, or to save an existing file in a new location, with a different name, or as a different file type.

ScreenTip
A brief explanation of a button or object that appears when the mouse pointer is paused over it. Other ScreenTips are accessed by clicking What's This? on the Help menu and then clicking a particular item, or by clicking the question mark button in the Title bar of dialog boxes.

Scroll bar
A graphical device for moving vertically and horizontally through a document with the mouse. Scroll bars are located along the right and bottom edges of the document window.

Search and replace
See Find and replace.

Section
A part of a document separated from the rest of the document by a section break. By separating a document into sections, you can use different page and column formatting in different parts of the same document.

Selection bar
An invisible column at the left edge of a column of text used to select text with the mouse. In a table, each cell has its own Selection bar at the left edge of the cell.

Serif font
A font that has small strokes at the ends of the characters. Times New Roman and Palatino are serif fonts.

Show/Hide button
Turns on and off the display of nonprinting characters such as formatting, space, and paragraph marks.

Sizing handles
Small boxes at the corners or edge midpoints of a chart, graphic, or other object to click and drag with the mouse pointer to change the dimensions of the object.

Smart Tag
Enables you to perform external actions on types of data that Word recognizes such as names, e-mail addresses, and Web addresses. Items with Smart Tags are underlined with purple dots on the screen.

Soft return
A line break created by pressing [Shift]+[Enter]. This creates a new line without creating a new paragraph.

Sort order
The sequence in which you arrange text or data in a table; **ascending** order arranges from the start to end of the alphabet, lowest to highest number, or earliest to latest date; **descending** order arranges in the opposite direction.

Source file
A file that you transfer to a destination file—for example, a table from Excel or Access that you insert in a business report in Word.

Spreadsheet program
A software program used for calculations and financial analysis.

Standard toolbar
A row of buttons that perform some of the most frequently used commands, such as Open, Print and Save. Usually located under the menu bar.

Status bar
Located at the bottom of the Word window, it displays the current page number and section number, the total number of pages in the document, and the vertical position of the insertion point. It also indicates whether certain options are active.

Style
A group of formatting instructions that you name and store, and are able to modify. When you apply a style to selected characters and paragraphs, all the formatting instructions of that style are applied at once.

Style dialog box
A feature that allows you to examine the overall formatting and styles used in a document template. You can also preview your document formatted in the styles from a selected template.

Tab stop
A measured position for placing and aligning text at a specific distance along a line. Word has four kinds of tab stops, left-aligned (the default), centered, right-aligned, and decimal. Tab stops are shown on the horizontal ruler.

Table
One or more rows of cells commonly used to display numbers and other data for quick reference and analysis. Items in a table are organized into rows and columns. You can convert text into a table with the Insert Table command on the Table menu.

Task Pane
A new feature to Word that organizes common Word tasks in one pane that is convenient to access on the screen. Numerous Task Panes are available including New Document, Basic Search, Clipboard, and Reveal Formatting.

Template
A special kind of document that provides basic tools and text for creating a document. Templates can contain styles, AutoText items, macros, customized menu and key assignments, and text or graphics that are the same in different types of documents.

Thesaurus
A Word feature that supplies a list of synonyms (words with similar meanings) and antonyms (words with opposite meanings) for a word selected in a document.

Title bar
The horizontal bar at the top of a window that displays the name of the document or application that appears in that window.

Toolbar
A graphical bar containing several buttons that act as shortcuts for many common Word commands.

Undo
A command that lets you reverse previous actions or changes, usually editing or formatting actions. Actions from the File menu cannot be reversed. You can undo multiple actions by using the Undo drop-down list.

URL
An acronym for Uniform Resource Locator; an address specifying where a particular piece of information can be found. A Web address is a kind of URL.

Value
In tables, data consisting of numbers (see also Label).

Vertical alignment
The placement of text on a page in relation to the top, bottom, or center of the page.

Vertical ruler
A graphical bar displayed at the left edge of the document window in Print Layout view. You can use this ruler to adjust the top and bottom page margins, and change row height in a table.

View
A display that shows certain aspects of the document. Word has seven views: Normal, Print Layout, Outline, Web Layout, Master Document, Full Screen, and Print Preview.

View buttons
Appear in the horizontal scroll bar. Allow you to display the document in one of four views: Normal, Print Layout, Web Layout, and Outline.

Window
A rectangular area on the screen in which you view and work on documents.

Windows Explorer

The powerful two-paned file management tool of the Windows operating system.

Winword.exe

The executable file stored on your hard drive or on a network server that actually runs Microsoft Word. When you launch Word from the Start menu, you are actually using a shortcut to this file.

Wizard

A helpful program you use to create documents. When you use a wizard to create a document, you are asked a series of questions about document preferences and content, and then the wizard creates the document to meet your specifications.

Word processing program

Software used to create documents efficiently. Usually includes features beyond simple editing, such as formatting and arranging text and graphics to create attractive documents.

Word Wrap

Feature that allows text you are typing to continue on the next line when you run out of space on the current line.

World Wide Web

A major component of the Internet, which is a vast global network of smaller networks and personal computers. Web pages include hyperlinks and present information in a graphical format that can incorporate text, graphics, sounds, and digital movies.

WYSIWYG

An acronym for What You See Is What You Get; indicates that a document will print out with the same formatting that is displayed in the document window.

Z

Zoom box

The rightmost box on the Standard toolbar for setting the percentage of enlargement of a document in the document window; Normal View default settings range from 10% to 500%.

index

a

Active window, WD 3.14-3.15
Alignment in tables, WD 4.6
Alignment of tabs, WD 3.8-3.9
Alignment of text, WD 1.14-1.15
Antonyms, finding, WD 3.30
Application window, WD 1.4-1.5
Application window Control icon, WD 1.9
Arrow keys, WD 1.12-1.13
AutoCorrect Exceptions dialog box, WD 3.22-3.24
AutoCorrect feature, WD 3.22-3.25
AutoFit, WD 4.4
AutoFormatting tables, WD 4.16-4.17
Automatic Spell Checking, WD 1.6, WD 3.18-3.21
AutoNumber option for footnotes, WD 3.6
AutoText, WD 3.26-3.29

b

Backspace key, WD 1.12
Bolding text, WD 1.14
Borders, WD 4.26-4.29
Break dialog box, WD 3.12-3.13

c

Calculating data in tables, WD 4.12-4.15
Cell markers, WD 4.3
Cell references, WD 4.14
Centered text, WD 1.15
Charts, WD 4.18-4.21
Clipboard, WD 2.6-2.7
Clipboard Task Pane, WD 2.6-2.7
Close button, WD 1.9
Closing documents, WD 1.8-1.9
Color, changing, WD 1.14
Columns, WD 4.2
Commands, WD 1.4
Continuous section break, WD 3.12-3.13
Convert table to text, text to table, WD 4.4
Copy button, WD 2.6, 2.22
Copying and moving text, WD 2.6-2.9
Copying and pasting text, WD 2.6, 3.14
Copying formats, WD 3.16-3.17
Copying text, WD 2.6-2.9
Create New Folder button, WD 1.8
Custom Dictionary, WD 3.21-3.22
Cut button, WD 2.6, 2.22
Cutting and pasting text, WD 2.6-2.7

d

Datasheet, WD 4.18-4.21
Deleting rows and columns, in tables, WD 4.8-4.9
Deleting text, WD 1.12-1.13, 2.6-2.7
Destination files, WD 4.4
Document window, WD 1.4-1.5
Documents:
   closing, WD 1.8-1.9
   editing, WD 1.12-13, 2.4-2.18
   footnotes and endnotes in, WD 3.6-3.7
   formatting, WD 1.14-1.15, 3.1-3.17
   indents in, WD 3.8-3.9
   line spacing in, WD 3.10-3.11
   moving through, WD 15, 1.12
   multiple, WD 3.14-3.15
   new, WD 1.6, 2.14
   opening, WD 1.10-1.11
   page breaks in, WD 3.12-3.13
   page numbers in, WD 3.4-3.5
   saving, WD 1.8-1.9
   section breaks in, WD 3.12-3.13
   setting margins in, WD 3.2-3.3
   tables in, WD 4.1-4.17
Drag-and-drop method, WD 2.8-2.9
Draw Table tool, WD 4.22-4.25

e

Edit menu, WD 2.6
Editing:
   with AutoCorrect, WD 3.22-3.25
   documents, WD 1.12-1.13, 2.1-2.17
   tables, WD 4.6-4.7
Embedded objects, WD 4.4
End key, WD 1.12-1.13
Endnotes, inserting, WD 3.6-3.7
Enter key, WD 1.6-1.7
Entering text, WD 1.6-1.7
Eraser button, WD 4.24
Excel, WD 4.4
Extensions, file name, WD 1.8

f

File names, WD 1.8
Files:
   destination and source, WD 4.4
   opening different formats, WD 1.10
   searching for, WD 2.2-2.3
Finding and Replacing text, WD 3.32-3.33
First line indent marker, WD 3.8
Font, defined, WD 1.14
Font box, WD 1.4
Font Color button, WD 1.14
Font size drop-down list, WD 1.14-1.15
Footnote and Endnote dialog box, WD 3.6-3.7
Format Painter, using, WD 3.16-3.17
Formatting, WD 1.14-1.15, 3.1-3.17
   tables, WD 4.4, 4.16-4.17
Formatting toolbar, WD 1.4-1.5, 1.14-1.15
Formulas, in tables, WD 4.12-4.15

g

Grammar checking, WD 3.18-3.21
Graphs, creating, WD 4.18-4.21
Gridlines, WD 4.2

h

Hanging indents, WD 3.8-3.9
Hard page break, WD 3.12
Headers/footers, WD 3.1-3.2, 3.4
Help button, WD 2.20
Help facility, WD 2.18-2.21
Hide/show white space, WD 3.12
Highlight button, WD 1.14
Highlight noncontiguous areas, WD 4.29
Home key, WD 1.12-1.13
Horizontal ruler, WD 1.5, 3.8-3.9
Horizontal scroll bar, WD 1.5

i

I-beam, WD 1.4
Inactive windows, WD 3.14-3.15
Insert Table button, WD 4.2-4.4

Inserting rows, columns, and cells in tables, WD 4.8-4.9
Inserting text, WD 1.12-1.13
Insertion point, WD 1.4-1.5, 1.12
   moving, WD 1.13
Italic button, WD 1.14

j

Justified text, WD 1.15

k

Keyboard, WD 1.12-1.13

l

Language dialog box, WD 3.20
Left-aligned text, WD 1.15
Line spacing, changing, WD 3.10-3.11
Linked objects, WD 4.4

m

Magnification tool, WD 1.16-1.17
Magnifier button, WD 1.16
Manual page break, WD 3.12
Margins, setting in documents, WD 3.2-3.3
Maximize button, WD 1.9
Menu bar, WD 1.4-1.5
Merging cells, WD 4.2, 4.24
Microsoft Graph, WD 4.18-4.21
Minimize button, WD 1.9
Mouse:
   drag and drop with, WD 2.8-2.9
   Selecting text with, WD 1.14, 2.4-2.5
Moving around documents, WD 1.12-1.13
Moving text, WD 2.6-2.9
Multiple Pages button, WD 1.16

n

New Document button, WD 1.4-1.5, 1.18
New Document Task Pane, WD 1.6-1.7
New features in Word XP:
   Hide/show white space, WD 3.12
   Highlight noncontiguous areas, WD 4.29
   Smart Tags, WD 1.6, 3.24
   Sort tables by more than one field name/column, WD 4.10

Nonprinting characters, WD 2.20-2.21, 3.16
Normal template, WD 2.14
Normal View, WD 3.4
Note pane, WD 3.6-3.7
Note reference mark, WD 3.7
Number format, WD 4.13-4.14
Num Lock key, WD 1.12, 2.4

o

Objects, embedded and linked, WD 4.4
Office Assistant, WD 2.18-2.20
Office Assistant dialog box, 2.18-2.19
Outline View, WD 3.4
Open button, WD 1.10, 2.2
Open dialog box, WD 1.10-1.11, 2.2-2.3
Opening existing files, WD 1.10-1.11
Options dialog box, WD 3.20-3.21
Outline View, WD 3.4
Overtype mode and button, WD 1.5, 1.12

p

Page breaks, inserting, WD 3.12-3.13
Page layout, defining, WD 3.2
Page numbers, inserting, WD 3.4-3.5
Page Numbers dialog box, WD 3.4-3.5
Page Setup dialog box, WD 3.2-3.3
Page Up, Page Down keys, WD 1.12-1.13
Paper size, selecting, WD 3.2
Paper source, selecting, WD 3.2
Paragraph:
   dialog box, WD 3.8-3.11
   formatting, WD 3.10
   indents, WD 3.8-3.9
Paragraph mark, WD 3.16
Paste button and command, WD 2.6-2.7
Paste Options button, WD 2.6
Placeholders, WD 2.12-2.14
Points, for type size, WD 1.14
Preview area, WD 2.10-2.11, 3.2-3.3, 3.10-3.11, 4.26-4.27
Print button, WD 1.16
Print dialog box, WD 1.16-1.17
Print Layout View, WD 1.4, 3.4, 3.6
Print Preview, WD 1.16-1.17
Printing, WD 1.16-1.17
Programs menu, WD 1.2-1.3

r

Recently used files, 1.10, 3.14
Redo button, WD 2.4, 2.22
Redo command, WD 2.4, 2.22

Repeat command, WD 2.4, 2.22, 4.28-4.29
Replace command, WD 3.32
Restore button, WD 1.9
Résumé Wizard, WD 2.10-2.13
Right-aligned text, WD 1.15
Rows and columns, in tables, WD 4.6-4.9
Ruler, WD 1.4-1.5
   and indents, WD 3.8-3.9

s

Save As dialog box, WD 1.8-1.9
Save command, WD 1.8
Saving documents, WD 1.8-1.9
ScreenTips, WD 1.4, 2.20, 3.17
Scroll bar arrows, WD 1.5
Scroll bar boxes, WD 1.5
Searching for files, WD 2.2-2.3
Searching for words, WD 3.32-3.33
Section breaks, WD 3.12-3.13
Selecting documents, WD 1.14
Selecting text, WD 1.14-1.15, 2.4-2.5
Shading, WD 4.26-4.29
Shading Color button, WD 4.28
Show/Hide button, WD 2.20-2.21, 3.16
Shrink to Fit, WD 1.16
Size box, WD 1.4
Sizing buttons, WD 1.9
Sizing handles, WD 4.20
Smart Tags, WD 1.6, 3.24
Soft page break, WD 3.12
Sort dialog box, WD 4.10-4.11
Sorting data in tables, WD 4.10-4.11
Source files, WD 4.4
Spacing in documents, WD 3.10-3.11
Spell checking, WD 1.6, 3.18-3.21
Spelling and Grammar dialog box, WD 3.18-3.21
Split cells, WD 4.3
Standard toolbar, WD 1.4-1.5
Start button, WD 1.2
Status bar, WD 1.5
Synonyms, finding, WD 3.30-3.31

t

Tab key:
   indenting with, WD 3.8
   and Tables, WD 4.6-4.7
Tabs, WD 4.4
Table AutoFormat dialog box, WD 4.16-4.17
Tables:
   calculating data in, WD 4.12-4.15
   and Columns, WD 4.8-4.10
   creating, WD 4.1-4.5, 4.22-4.25

editing, WD 4.6-4.7
   formatting, WD 4.4, 4.16-4.17
   formulas in, WD 4.12-4.15
   inserting and deleting rows, WD 4.8-4.9
   sorting data in, WD 4.10-4.11
Table Properties dialog box, WD 4.16, 4.26
Tables and Borders toolbar, WD 4.4-4.5, 4.22, 4.24, 4.28
Task Pane, WD 1.4-1.7, 2.6-2.7, 2.20
Templates, using, WD 2.14-2.17
Text:
   alignment of, WD 1.15
   centered, WD 1.15
   cutting, copying, moving, WD 2.6-2.9
   deleting, WD 1.12-1.13
   entering, WD 1.6-1.7
   finding and replacing, WD 3.32-3.33
   fonts, WD 1.14
   inserting, WD 1.12-1.13
   justified, WD 1.15
   selecting, WD 1.14-1.15, 2.4-2.5
   size of, WD 1.14
   typing over, WD 1.12

Text Direction button, WD 4.24
Thesaurus feature, using, WD 3.30-3.31
Title bar, WD 1.4-1.5
Toolbars submenu, WD 1.4
Typeface, WD 1.14

U

Underline button, WD 1.14, 4.24
Undo button, WD 1.12, 2.4, 2.22
Undoing actions, WD 1.12, 2.4-2.5
Update Fields command, WD 4.14

V

Values, WD 4.2
Vertical scroll bar, WD 1.5
View buttons, WD 1.4-1.5, 3.4
Viewing documents, WD 3.4

W

Web Layout View, WD 3.4
What's This? command, WD 2.20-2.21
Windows Clipboard, WD 2.6
Windows desktop, WD 1.3
Windows Start menu, WD 1.2-1.3
Wizards, using, WD 2.10-2.13
Word:
   commands, WD 1.4
   screen, WD 1.2-1.5
   starting, WD 1.2-1.3
Word Count dialog box, WD 3.30-3.31
Word Wrap, WD 1.6

Z

Zoom box, WD 1.16

FILE DIRECTORY

The table below summarizes the external data files that have been provided for the student. Many of the exercises in this book cannot be completed without these files. The files are distributed as part of the Instructor's Resource Kit and are also available for download at http://www.mhhe.com/it/cit/index.mhtml. Please note that the table below only lists the raw files that are provided, not the versions students are instructed to save after making changes to the raw files nor new files that the students create themselves.

Lesson	Skill Name/Page #	File Name	Introduced In
Lesson 1	Opening an Existing Document/WD 1.10	wddoit1-5.doc	do it! step 4
	Opening an Existing Document/WD 1.11	wdprac1-5.doc	Practice
	Deleting and Inserting Text/WD 1.12	wddoit1-6.doc	do it! step 1
	Deleting and Inserting Text/WD 1.13	wdprac1-6.doc	Practice
	Formatting Text/WD 1.14	wddoit1-7.doc	do it! step 1
	Formatting Text/WD 1.15	wdprac1-7.doc	Practice
	Previewing and Printing a Document/WD 1.16	wddoit1-8.doc	do it! step 1
	Previewing and Printing a Document/WD 1.17	wdprac1-8.doc	Practice
	Interactivity/WD 1.21	wdskills1.doc	Build Your Skills #2
Lesson 2	Searching for Files/WD 2.2	wddoit2-1.doc	do it! step 6
	Searching for Files/WD 2.3	wdprac2-1.doc	Practice
	Selecting Text and Undoing Actions/WD 2.4	wddoit2-2.doc	do it! step 1
	Selecting Text and Undoing Actions/WD 2.5	wdprac2-2.doc	Practice
	Cutting, Copying, and Moving Text/WD 2.6	wddoit2-3.doc	do it! step 1
	Cutting, Copying, and Moving Text/WD 2.7	wdprac2-3.doc	Practice
	Copying and Moving Text with the Mouse/WD 2.8	wddoit2-4.doc	do it! step 1
	Copying and Moving Text with the Mouse/WD 2.9	wdprac2-4.doc	Practice
	Interactivity/WD 2.25	wdskills2.doc	Build Your Skills #1
Lesson 3	Setting Up a Page/WD 3.2	wddoit3-1.doc	do it! step 1
	Setting Up a Page/WD 3.3	wdprac3-1.doc	Practice
	Inserting Page Numbers/WD 3.4	wddoit3-2.doc	do it! step 1
	Inserting Page Numbers/WD 3.5	wdprac3-2.doc	Practice
	Inserting Endnotes and Footnotes/WD 3.6	wddoit3-3.doc	do it! step 1
	Inserting Endnotes and Footnotes/WD 3.7	wdprac3-3.doc	Practice
	Applying Paragraph Indents/WD 3.8	wddoit3-4.doc	do it! step 1
	Applying Paragraph Indents/WD 3.9	wdprac3-4.doc	Practice
	Changing Line Spacing/WD 3.10	wddoit3-5.doc	do it! step 1
	Changing Line Spacing/WD 3.11	wdprac3-5.doc	Practice
	Inserting Page Breaks/WD 3.12	wddoit3-6.doc	do it! step 1
	Inserting Page Breaks/WD 3.13	wdprac3-6.doc	Practice
	Working with Multiple Documents/WD 3.14	wddoit3-7.doc	do it! step 1
	Working with Multiple Documents/WD 3.14	wddoit3-7a.doc	do it! step 1
	Working with Multiple Documents/WD 3.15	wdprac3-7.doc	Practice
	Working with Multiple Documents/WD 3.15	wdprac3-7a.doc	Practice
	Using the Format Painter/WD 3.16	wddoit3-8.doc	do it! step 1
	Using the Format Painter/WD 3.17	wdprac3-8.doc	Practice
	Checking Spelling and Grammar/WD 3.18	wddoit3-9.doc	do it! step 1
	Checking Spelling and Grammar/WD 3.19	wdprac3-9.doc	Practice
	Using AutoCorrect/WD 3.25	wdprac3-10.doc	Practice
	Inserting Frequently Used Text/WD 3.29	wdprac3-11.doc	Practice
	Using the Word Thesaurus/WD 3.30	wddoit3-12.doc	do it! step 1
	Using the Word Thesaurus/WD 3.31	wdprac3-12.doc	Practice
	Finding and Replacing Text/WD 3.32	wddoit3-13.doc	do it! step 1
	Finding and Replacing Text/WD 3.33	wdprac3-13.doc	Practice

Lesson	Skill Name/Page #	File Name	Introduced In
Lesson 3	Interactivity/WD 3.37	wdskills3.doc	Build Your Skills #1
	Interactivity/WD 2.37	wdskills3a.doc	Build Your Skills #4
	Interactivity/WD 3.38	wdproblem3.doc	Problem Solving #1
	Interactivity/WD 3.38	wdproblem3a.doc	Problem Solving #1
Lesson 4	Creating and Modifying Tables/WD 4.2	wddoit4-1.doc	do it! step 1
	Creating and Modifying Tables/WD 4.5	wdprac4-1.doc	Practice
	Editing Tables/WD 4.6	wddoit4-2.doc	do it! step 1
	Editing Tables/WD 4.7	wdprac4-2.doc	Practice
	Inserting and Deleting Rows, Columns, and Cells/WD 4.8	wddoit4-3.doc	do it! step 1
	Inserting and Deleting Rows, Columns, and Cells/WD 4.9	wdprac4-3.doc	Practice
	Sorting Data in a Table/WD 4.10	wddoit4-4.doc	do it! step 1
	Sorting Data in a Table/WD 4.11	wdprac4-4.doc	Practice
	Calculating Data in a Table/WD 4.12	wddoit4-5.doc	do it! step 1
	Calculating Data in a Table/WD 4.15	wdprac4-5.doc	Practice
	Formatting a Table/WD 4.16	wddoit4-6.doc	do it! step 1
	Formatting a Table/WD 4.17	wdprac4-6.doc	Practice
	Creating a Chart/WD 4.18	wddoit4-7.doc	do it! step 1
	Creating a Chart/WD 4.19	wdprac4-7.doc	Practice
	Editing a Chart/WD 4.20	wddoit4-8.doc	do it! step 1
	Editing a Chart/WD 4.21	wdprac4-8.doc	Practice
	Adding Borders and Shading/WD 4.26	wddoit4-9.doc	do it! step 1
	Adding Borders and Shading/WD 4.29	mywdprac4-6.doc	Practice

NOTES

NOTES

NOTES